D0898403

THE SOLENT WAY

A Guide to
Hampshire's Coast

BARRY SHURLOCK

HAMPSHIRE COUNTY COUNCIL
Recreation Department

For Jonathan and Sally

Acknowledgements

I am most grateful to the many individuals, too numerous to be named, who kindly supplied information, particularly the curators of the many museums on the Hampshire coast.

I would like to give special thanks to Mrs Philippa Stevens, Local Studies Librarian at the Winchester District Library, who gave much helpful advice on sources.

My editor has been John Holder of the County Recreation Department, who invited me to write this book, proposed the layout and organisation of the material and made many helpful suggestions.

Barry Shurlock
Abbot's Worthy, Hampshire

Published by Hampshire County Recreation, North Hill Close, Andover Road, Winchester, Hampshire.

Designed by David Cradduck Graphic Design Services, Laurel House, Station Approach, Alresford, Hampshire.

Printed by Borcombe Printers Ltd., Unit 6, Budds Lane, Romsey, Hampshire.

ISBN 0 905392 40X

THE SOLENT WAY

Foreword

Hampshire is rich in tourist attractions with countryside and coastline of great natural beauty and a variety of historical heritage that few other counties can match.

The Solent Way Long Distance Coastal Path was established by the County Council in 1982. Passing coastal marshes and river mouths, beaches and shingle spits, visiting castles, ships and museums, stopping in riverside villages and in towns, it crosses through the historic ports and makes occasional ferry passages. The route includes a taste of the New Forest and for much of the time enjoys views of the Isle of Wight.

The Solent Way is an unforgetable experience. A coastal path it may be, but it is really much more — perhaps the best description would be "an invitation to discover Hampshire".

Barry Shurlock's fascinating story of our shores, and the excellent walking which the route offers combine to make an ideal introduction to our maritime Country. Here then is a wonderful chance to explore some more of Hampshire, with 60 miles of natural and historic heritage and sheer delight!

Councillor C.M. Jones M.A. (Cantab.)
Chairman, Recreation Committee
Hampshire County Council

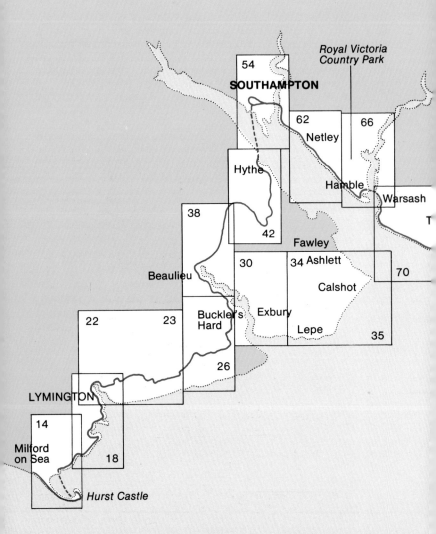

The Solent Way

WAY

Royal Victoria
Country Park

54

SOUTHAMPTON

62   66
Netley

Hythe   Hamble
                        Warsash
38   T
        42
Fawley
30   34 Ashlett
Beaulieu   70
              Calshot
Buckler's Exbury
Hard
22   23   Lepe
                        35
        26

LYMINGTON

14
Milford
on Sea   18

Hurst Castle

Contents

I Milford-on-Sea to Lymington   7
II Lymington to Bucklers Hard   19
III Exbury to Fawley   29
IV Beaulieu to Hythe   37
V Southampton   47
VI Woolston to Hamble   57
VII Hamble to Titchfield   65
VIII Hill Head to Gosport   77
IX Portsmouth   87
X Southsea, Eastney & Hayling Island 97
XI Langstone Harbour and Emsworth   105
Information Pages   117
Further Reading   127
Index   129

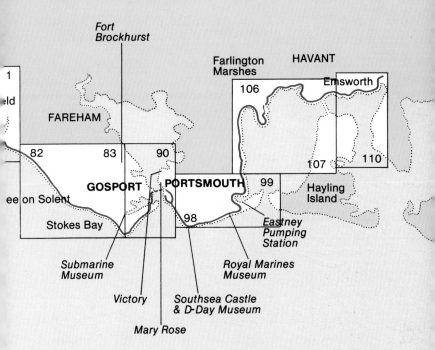

Maps reproduced from the 1983 Ordnance Survey 1 : 25000 map
with the permission of the Controller of Her Majesty's Stationery Office,
Crown Copyright reserved.

MILFORD-ON-SEA
TO
LYMINGTON

Hurst Castle

MILFORD-ON-SEA TO LYMINGTON

One of the pleasantest things in the world is going a journey

William Hazlitt

Before the Isle of Wight was separated from the mainland the land of Milford-on-Sea was several miles to the north of the banks of the Solent River, a huge waterway which ran east before turning to join the English Channel.

The steady erosion which first hove off England from the Continent and then created the Isle of Wight is still at work. Indeed, until the early years of the last century Milford-on-Sea was an inland parish kept from having a seaboard by a narrow strip of Hordle, the parish to the west, which then included Hurst Castle spit.

So soft are the cliffs hereabouts that in the latter half of the eighteenth century as much as a quarter of a mile of land was lost and — hey presto! — Milford-on-Sea got a seafront.

Milford, as it is called locally, made the most of its newly acquired coastline when in 1887 the local landowner, Colonel William Cornwallis West, whose family seat was nearby at Newlands Manor, decided to create a seaside resort. He made his intentions clear by adding 'on-sea' to the name and land was sold to the many people who wanted to live and retire on the South Coast.

The seafront which eventually grew up is said by Pevsner to reflect architectural styles 'from Norman-Shavian half-timbered gables and tile-hanging to neo-Georgian'.

Today, Milford is a pleasant residential town that springs to life in the summer and slumbers for the rest of the year. But ambitions for it to become a sort of mini-Brighton were never even remotely realised.

The Solent Way starts on the seafront, but before setting out, the walker should explore the church, whose stubby steeple beckons above the housetops alongside the triangular village green.

All Saints church was built by the Normans on an earlier Saxon foundation. As you enter the porch you see arches which date from 1150-70, with beautifully carved capitals to the pillars.

More arches flank the nave, some supported by columns of Purbeck stone. The tracery about the stained glass windows is reminiscent of the famous priory at Christchurch.

There are memorials to members of the Cornwallis West family, including 'Theresa John, authoress, 1806-86', who sadly has been ignored by the editors of reference books.

And in the north-west window of the chancel is a stained glass panel showing Charles I, who was imprisoned nearby in Hurst castle.

As you leave the church a large stone cross stands ahead: it was res-

The Needles, opposite Milford sea front

tored in 1864 by the widow of a quixotic wildfowler and diarist, Colonel Peter Hawker, whose spirit still lurks amidst the marshes of Keyhaven.

All Saints is notable for the dissension of one of its clergymen, the Rev. Harrington Evans, who in 1816 with many of his congregation deserted the established church and built a Baptist chapel, which still stands in Milford, in Barnes Lane.

Returning to the Solent Way, just after leaving the green you cross over a rather muddy river that flows to the east. We shall meet it again — but note its name, the Danes Stream. According to legend, it was called after a bloody battle.

The seafront at Milford gives a lovely view of the Isle of Wight — the Needles and the green hills backed by the heights of Tennyson Down. The Hampshire-Dorset border is only a few miles to the west, at Highcliffe, in the centre of the huge sweep of Christchurch Bay which ends at the stack of Hengistbury Head.

But note also the sea: here it flows with the full force of the Channel and the beach-huts and prom regularly get half-buried in shingle.

The huge piles of rock which have been heaped up to the east of the seafront are there to minimise erosion. And an embankment prevents the sea from swamping Sturt Pond, which lies behind the shore and is fed by the Danes Stream.

Until Milford became a resort its local people used to earn a living by dredging for stone scoured out by the sea. Soft grey nodules called septaria were used for making Roman cement, which sets under water.

Ironstone was also gathered locally for smelting at the ironworks at Sowley, beyond Lymington. So profitable was the activity, apparently, that people deserted the harvest fields for the shore.

The coast at Milford and Hordle still recalls this open-cast mining and is called the Mineway.

Hurst Castle from the spit

And Hordle cliff to the west, it should be mentioned, is world famous for stone of a different sort — fossils, which so delighted the Victorians. The soft earth of this shore has yielded up the bones of crocodile and alligator.

From Sturt Pond the Danes Stream runs in a straight cut to emerge alongside **Hurst Castle spit**.

This huge bank of pebbles, a mile and a half long and reaching halfway to the Isle of Wight, is the largest example of a feature which is typical of the Hampshire coastline.

For centuries Hurst has been built up layer by layer by longshore drifting. And from time to time the same forces which have made it have overrun it and breached it, allowing the marshes to the east to be flooded.

To conserve the spit, vast quantities of stone (some of it rubble from the former Royal Victoria Hospital, Netley) have been laid down.

Walking the spit is a bit like climbing a mountain on the flat. The bare pebble ridge is virtually barren, with the exception of patches of sea-kale and poppy. But the mass of Hurst Castle and its lighthouses provide a constant goal.

The central part of the castle dates from Tudor times and was built by Henry VIII at a time when fears of invasion led to a great strengthening of coastal defences. Several new castles were built on the Solent at this time, including one at Yarmouth on the Isle of Wight.

The Tudor castle consists of a 12-sided central tower with three rounded bastions. The long wings which flank the old building provided a formidable firepower to sea and were added in the 1870s when there were renewed fears of French aggression.

The castle was originally manned by a governor and 23 men, though in Victorian times its garrison was large enough to support an inn.

The two lighthouses on Hurst, the white 'high light' and the red 'low light' provide essential aids for ships entering the Solent from the west.

Hurst also used to have an 'electric telegraph' station, set up in 1854, it is said, as a convenience for the royal household at Osborne House. One officer became so attached to the place that in 25 years of service he only left the spit once.

Others have been kept at Hurst against their will, notably Charles I, whose 19-day stay in 1648 gave the castle a place in national history. Father Paul Atkinson, a Franciscan, is also remembered (and has given rise to ghost stories). At a time of anti-Popery his religious views led to his incarceration on Hurst from 1700 until his death 29 years later.

Hurst was used briefly for curing herring, but a far more important 'industry' in this part of Hampshire was smuggling. French brandy was brought over in small cutters and 'worked up' into the New Forest. Tales abound of men in the night who 'borrowed' farmers' wagons and, of course, returned them in due course.

The farmer's recompense was a tub of brandy, called a blackbird, which would be left at the back door.

There is no doubt that smuggling was an important source of income for people living on a remote coast beyond easy reach of the law. But as

Keyhaven Harbour

the revenue men improved their tactics the business occasionally turned very nasty.

Locally there was a notable battle which took place on Milford Green in 1781 and later clashes often involved the Militia stationed at Lymington. A ripping yarn which gives a flavour of the times, and is based on Christchurch, is *The Smugglers of Haven Quay*, by F.J. Vallings, published in 1911.

From Hurst the Solent Way continues by ferry, the first of four on the trail. The small boat wends its way amidst the mudflats and floating sheets of green weed into **Keyhaven Harbour.**

It is a small harbour with a scatter of working boats and the sailing craft of the Keyhaven Yacht Club and the Hurst Castle Sailing Club. At its head is the Avon Water, which old maps show used to turn eastward about half a mile inland and flow as twin streams across Keyhaven marshes: the marks of the former course are still there. Above the harbour sluice gates the river is flanked by extensive beds of reed, which give shelter to many birds.

One of Keyhaven's most notable characters is Colonel Peter Hawker, whose memorial we have already noted in the churchyard at Milford.

Hawker lived on the Test at Longparish but spent much of his time at Keyhaven, where he set off to stalk wildfowl on the marshes that stretch to Lymington and beyond. In the village pub, The Gun Inn, are some pictures which show how he did it: lying in a punt with a huge gun.

Often going out in bitter weather, he would manoeuvre his craft until a 'raft' of birds was in the sights of the gun and then touch the trigger. His bags were prodigious. His published *Diary*, which oozes with the bloody gusto of the man, shows that during the period 1802-53 he killed 29 species of bird, including 1,327 brent geese.

Hawker's cottage, which he called his 'little gunning place', can still be seen next to The Gun Inn. And the channel that runs from the open sea into the harbour is called Hawker's Lake.

15

Eight Acre Pond, Salterns Sailing Club

Keyhaven is one of the most pleasant places to be on a summer's day, but it might have been otherwise. Before the First World War two schemes were put forward that would have changed it dramatically — one to bore a tunnel to the Isle of Wight and another to build a docks system on the marshes to the east.

As it happens, Keyhaven, Pennington and Oxey marshes are industrial relics of a different kind, for they were created, preserved and eventually given up as wasteland by the owners of the vast number of salterns which used to be worked on this shore when the Lymington salt industry was of national significance.

Now it is one of the finest stretches of marshlands to be found anywhere — a huge nature reserve which supports a rich flora and a vast, shifting population of waders, wildfowl and many other types of birds.

After Keyhaven the Solent Way soon takes the course of a sea-wall nearly five miles long which runs almost all the way to Lymington. It was built to prevent the salterns from being swamped (its absence at Hurst led to the early demise of the industry there), for flooding became a serious problem on this part of the coast from the late eighteenth century. Engineering works have now made a flood reservoir out of the upper reaches of the Avon Water, but until very recently sandbags-at-the-ready was part of life at Keyhaven.

After rounding the southern margin of **Keyhaven Marshes**, just beyond the start of the built-up sea-wall, you will come across a large pond which is often alive with flocks of geese and other birds. It is the first hint of the birdwatcher's bonanza which continues now to Lymington. Apart from many native species, these grounds support large numbers of visitors and migratory birds.

In the autumn and winter there come redshank, dunlin and whimbrel from Iceland. There are also other species from Northern Scandinavia, such as spotted redshank, greenshank and ruff, while from Northern Russia come brent goose, curlew-sandpiper, little stint and grey plover.

Summer visitors from various parts of Africa include three species of tern — little, common and sandwich — and bar-tailed godwit, sanderling and arctic skua on Spring migration.

The most important nesting bird in the area is the little tern which nests in colonies offshore on the banks between **Pennington** and Lymington. But there are many other species of nesting bird on the marshes, including vast numbers of gulls. Indeed, black-headed gulls are so prolific that commercial harvesting of their eggs, a traditional local industry, is carried on during the early weeks of the season.

Any walker on the Lymington marshes is bound to be impressed by the wildlife of this wasteland, but equally he should be alert to the traces of the old salt industry which remain. The first mark can be seen close to the second kink in the straight-sided section of sea-wall after Keyhaven marshes. A gorse-covered mound in the middle of the marsh shows the site of one of the small windmills which pumped concentrated brine from shallow ponds on the marshes into boiling houses.

About a mile further on the path takes a turn around the northern end of **Oxey Marsh** and continues along a creek which gets progressively narrower., This is Moses Dock, one of the inlets which was used by the salt industry: coal for boiling came in and salt went out!

At the head of Moses Dock are some of the old brick buildings which were used and further on, beyond the Salterns Sailing Club is Maiden Dock, another relic of the days when the Lymington marshes in the summer months was lined with windmills and boiling houses in full swing.

At the end of the season the saltworkers were rewarded with a feast. Legs of lamb wrapped in dough were cooked in brine and served with garnishings of samphire picked from the marsh.

This part of the Hampshire coast was particularly suitable for salterns because the water flowed gently over the mudflats and could easily be contained in shallow ponds. From these it was baled into square enclosures with little mud walls, where it was further concentrated by evaporation. Alongside Maiden Dock, and at a number of places between here and Lymington, the lattice-like patterns of the old salt-pans can clearly be seen.

At its heyday the local salt industry produced about 6,000 tons a year, about 10 per cent of the total produced in the country. The Naval dockyard at Portsmouth consumed a good deal of this for salting meat and salt was also taken across the Atlantic to Newfoundland. Competition from mined salt and harsh taxation eventually made the Lymington salterns unprofitable and the last boiling house closed down in 1865.

Shotts Copse

Snooks
Farm

FB

13

Walhampton

Mon

Bampton's Farm

Lisle Court
Farm

Lisle Court

Cattle Grid

12

Sch

Sta

11

10

Marina

Sta

Ferry Terminal

5

Flushards

Horn Reach

Pylewell Lake

IRB.Sta

Pontoons

Yacht Haven

Waterford

Woodside
Gardens

Delawarr
House

NTL

Normandy Farm

Short Reach

Long Reach

Woodside

Saltworks

Lymington Sp

Normandy

Eight Acre
Pond

Sta

The Salterns

PH

Pipe Line

Narrow Mark

Oxey Marsh

Jack in the Basket

Oxey Lake

Mean High Water

nnington Marshes

Mean Low Water

Jetty

Pipe Line

Ferry (V)

LYMINGTON TO BUCKLERS HARD

Royal
Lymington Yacht Club

LYMINGTON TO BUCKLERS HARD

Lymington is in a manner insulated by the New Forest, which shuts it in on three sides . . .

Quoted by Edward King, 1900

The Solent Way reaches the **Lymington River** in style. After more than five miles of open marshland the path comes upon the wooded shore of the river opposite, with a few scattered yachts moored between the mudbanks and then leads straight into the heart of a marina.

There is a forest of masts and rigging and brightly coloured hulls, and a sound like an oriental street band made by steel ropes slapping against aluminium masts. Nearby are the premises of the Royal Lymington Yacht Club, a prestigious club with more than 2,000 members. It dates from the 1920s and like most of the more exclusive clubs it has an Admiralty Warrant, which allows it to fly the red ensign.

Note the faceted windowfront of the RLYC which gives its members a superb view of the river. But note also the Bath House nearby, built in 1833 and now the headquarters of the Lymington Sailing Club. Old prints show what an elegant building it used to be.

The open-air, saltwater baths themselves, which are on the site of King's Saltern, have an air of between-the-wars charm, complete with potted palms, though they were originally built at the same time as the Bath House.

At the back of the RLYC, where the RNLI have premises, is a huge lamp standard with two gaslights and an inscription which says that when the streets of Lymington were first lit by gas in 1832 the iron columns were given by one member of the Burrard family and the lamps by another. The slender elegant columns are still there, though electricity has replaced gas.

The Solent Way passes the yard of the Berthon Boat Co., a well-known local boatbuilding company which was given its name by the Rev. E. L. Berthon, a cleric who invented a number of nautical devices, including the screw propellor (though there are other claimants) and the collapsible boat — a sort of lifeboat made from canvas and wood that could be easily folded up and stowed.

Before Berthon the yard belonged to Thomas Inman, a notable boatbuilder from Hastings who set up in business at Lymington in 1819. His yachts were found to be almost unbeatable during the early years of racing, when the members of the Royal Yacht Squadron at Cowes often challenged one another on the waters of the Solent.

Inman brought to Lymington the beginnings of a business which has more than made up for the loss of the salt industry. Yachting is now its major activity. Not only does the river give harbour to more than 1,500 yachts, but a wide variety of nautical enterprises flourish: yacht

Town Quay, Lymington

designers, naval architects, sailmakers, chandleries and maritime writers and sailors-extraordinaire such as Clare Francis, who until recently lived in the town.

The heart of Lymington is the area around the old quay. But note also the High Street with the distinctive clock tower of St. Thomas's church jutting out at the top. The street still has something of the atmosphere of a fashionable resort, which Lymington was in the eighteenth century, when Rowlandson recorded its scenes in a series of drawings.

Today the river tends to be dominated by the Sealink car ferries which ply between Lymington Harbour Station and Yarmouth on the Isle of Wight. Tennyson composed one of this best known poems, *Crossing the Bar*, while he took the ferry on the way to his home near Freshwater.

The Solent Way crosses the river by way of a causeway which, it is said, has increased the silting-up of the estuary as well as preventing access to the upper reaches. It was built in 1731 by a retired merchant captain who claimed dubious rights to dam the river in this way and charge a toll for those who used it. Although vigorous opposition to the scheme rumbled on for many years, it was not until 1967 that the toll ceased.

On the outskirts of Lymington, at the top of a steep valley side, the trail passes a granite obelisk, which commemorates the achievements of Admiral Sir Harry Burrard Neale (he who gave the town iron columns), the most notable member of a family which dominated the politics and life of the town for two hundred years.

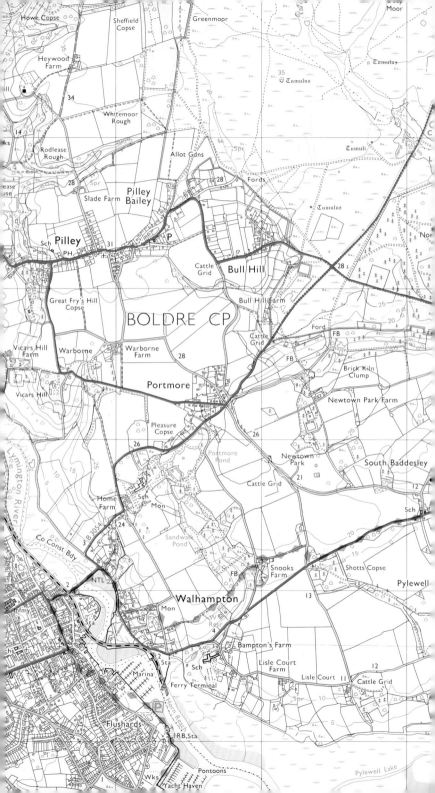

Burrard Neale Monument

Sir Harry lived at Walhampton House, which lies about half a mile to the north of the monument. Now a preparatory school, the present nineteenth century building replaced an earlier house built in 1711. Its splendid facade is soon seen from the path and at the same time another fine mansion, Elmer's Court, is visible to the south.

The Solent Way now stays inland until it reaches Southampton Water. It passes through some of the most pleasant forest scenery in Southern England. Most of the land is still held by large estates: mansion houses and scatters of cottages are all that will be seen for some miles.

From time to time there are glimpses of the Solent, but see if you agree with William Gilpin, sometime vicar of Boldre, who specifically writes about the views from Walhampton in his *Remarks on Forest Scenery*, published in 1791. He first comments that the views 'may rather be called *amusing* than *picturesque*'. Then he says: 'They are too extensive for the use of the pencil. The distant coast exhibits too long a curtain; hills are too smooth; and the water-line is too parallel with the coast of Hampshire.'

Gilpin is rather begrudging, but perhaps more trees have grown up since he was writing.

One mansion glimpsed from the Solent Way at Snooks Farm is Newton Park, a white house with a huge classical front. But far more important in this part of Hampshire is **Pylewell Park**, the first trace of which is seen at Shotts Copse. The mansion house itself is soon visible at the end of a drive lined with globose ornamental trees.

The Welds, a notable Catholic family, held Pylewell as a secondary house to their family seat, Lulworth Castle, in the early nineteenth century. The family helped emigrés, who sought refuge in Lymington after the French Revolution, to keep up their faith. A Catholic chapel was also built at Pylewell and one member of the family, Thomas Weld, became a cardinal.

The religious history of Pylewell is reflected in the church at **South Baddesley**, just off the route, which is almost bare with the exception of two brass tablets commemorating deeds of William Ingham Whitaker and his brother-in-law.

The Whitakers, who still live at Pylewell, bought the estate in the 1860s, after the death of Joseph Weld, whose racing successes with yachts built by Thomas Inman at Lymington led to the invention of the handicap systems which are used in yachting today.

Beyond South Baddesley is Pylewell Home Farm and its houses, which form a classic, modern estate village. Over the cattle grid at the edge of the village the Solent Way enters the New Forest. Ahead is Sowley Brooms, a beautiful wood of dying birch and small oaks and then **Sowley Pond**, an old fish-pond built by the Cistercian monks from Beaulieu Abbey. It is a beautiful expanse of water with huge Scots Pine growing at its edge. The heavily silted estuaries of the streams which were dammed to make the pond can be seen to the south.

In the 17th and 18th centuries, long after the dissolution, there was an important iron-works at Sowley. Beside the track which leads to

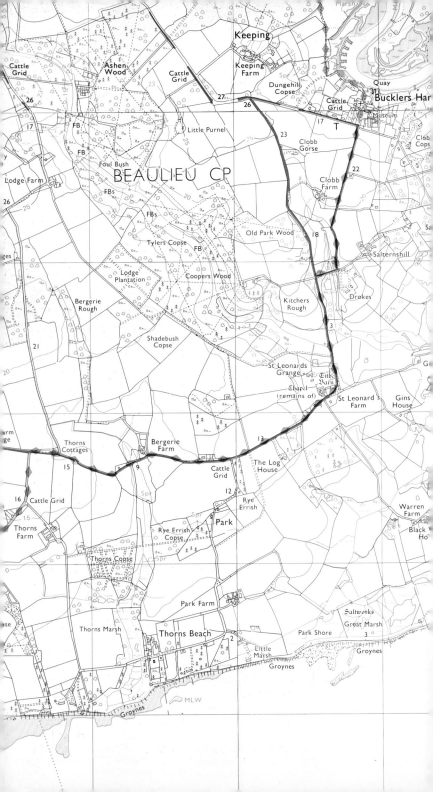

Model of shipbuilding at Bucklers Hard

Colgrims can be seen traces of reddened earth and slag from the old furnaces and forge. Ironstone from Hengistbury Head and Hordle Cliffs was smelted and worked in tilt-hammers powered by the waters of the pond. Nails for shipbuilding and guns for the East India Company were some of the products made.

The monks at Beaulieu worked their extensive lands according to the grange system. Lay brothers living on farms did all the agricultural work and the produce was either used by the monastic brethren or sold. At **St Leonard's Grange**, two miles on from Sowley, the remains of one of the huge barns used to store produce can still be seen. At a time when English wool was exported in vast quantities through Southampton, this barn was the central collecting store for all the wool produced on the Beaulieu estates. It was called a *bergerie*, from the Latin for sheep, a name which is remembered on a farm nearby.

The Solent Way meets the Beaulieu river at **Bucklers Hard**. Now a tourist attraction and the site of a maritime museum, this fragment of an 18th century model village is all the better for being thronged with visitors. It is almost possible to believe that the shipwrights who built men-of-war and merchant vessels here will appear at the doors of the cottages that line the main street.

Perhaps it was this feeling that encouraged the owner, Lord Montagu, to bring to life the New Inn and other parts of the village with the aid of life-size tableaux. The sounds of recorded, authentic conversations — and even a special system for injecting odours (hops, sweat and cooking smells!) add to the reality.

It may sound corny, but the interiors have been very carefully researched and are very realistic. At the bar of the New Inn you will see Charles Pocock, the Reading ironmaster who breathed new life into

27

Walkers leaving Bucklers Hard

Sowley iron-works and supplied the shipyard with nails. Standing rather uneasily near the fire-place is Nicholas Cory, the Salt Officer, whose job it was to levy taxes on the salt produced on the river.

The maritime museum itself gives the full story of the shipyard at Bucklers Hard, including a model of the yard and a display of the tools used by the shipwrights. From the middle of the 18th century until 1827 many large wooden vessels were constructed in launchways cut into the river bank. The best known was probably the *Agamemnon*, Nelson's favourite ship, which slid into the Beaulieu river in 1781.

Sir Francis Chichester, the epic single-handed yachtsman, used the river as a base when he successfully circumnavigated the globe in 160 days in 1966/7. His charts and other relics can be seen in the museum.

The Solent Way continues from Bucklers Hard along the east bank of the river to Beaulieu village. It is a walk through woodland with the river never far away. Mudbanks are held together with the roots of *Spartina*, which first colonised Southampton Water in the 1870s, but is now mysteriously beginning to die back. Sea lavender is common and there are large areas of this plant with its delicately coloured flowers. And there is a great deal more for the naturalist to see, for this is part of the North Solent National Nature Reserve, which recently became the first Area of Special Protection, as laid down by wildlife legislation.

The path now winds its way to **Baileys Hard** where the prominent chimney of an old brickworks can be seen. Just beyond, in a field which slopes down to the river, scenes from the film *A Man for All Seasons* were shot. If you have a chance to see it, look out for the shots of Sir Thomas More's 'Chelsea house', which were in fact made with an elaborate facade erected here on the banks of the Beaulieu river.

EXBURY
TO
FAWLEY

Fawley Power Station

Section III

EXBURY TO FAWLEY

HMS Mastodon was a stone frigate. It was Exbury Hall . . .

Nevile Shute, 1955

The world's finest collection of rhododendrons, a Roman harbour, fine country houses, a former RAF flying-boat station and an oil refinery — all these are to be found close to the shore that stretches between the lower reaches of the Beaulieu river and Hythe.

Although the Solent Way does not tread this coast — and note that there is no footpath along the whole length of the foreshore — it is an important part of Hampshire's Solent heritage.

Like most of the north-west Solent shore it is rather secretive. Much of it is privately owned and access to the sea has to be sought rather than being offered. This situation, though irksome to the walker, has preserved much of its natural beauty and its wildlife.

Gull Island at the entrance to the Beaulieu river holds the largest gull colony in the country. So many black-headed and herring gulls come back each year to build their nest in the shingle of the island that their eggs are deliberately destroyed and collected commercially to provide room for the rarer species that nest here, especially the terns — little, sandwich and common.

Other birds that nest in the mouth of the estuary include Canada geese and shelduck, and there are sightings of many rarer species, such as the mediterranean gull and even the osprey.

The best way to see the birds is by boat. The catamaran cruiser *Swiftsure* operates a regular sightseeing service from Bucklers Hard.

Although the river is today the most peaceful, least crowded inlet on the Solent, in 1944 it was the scene of hectic preparations for D-Day. Just below the traditional shipbuilding centre of Bucklers Hard, in a cut now marked with driven piles, parts of the Mulberry harbours were constructed before being towed into position on the coasts of Normandy.

And on the Lepe foreshore there was a slipway for landing craft, which were packed into the river. Nevil Shute has faithfully described the feverish work that was done at this time in *Requiem for a Wren*: even the shooting down of a plane included in the story took place. It landed in the gardens of Exbury House, where the Naval establishment HMS *Mastodon* had its headquarters.

Today **Exbury** has returned to the business it knows best, breeding rhododendrons. The hundreds of varieties which can be seen there are the result of more than 60 years' careful crossing and cultivation. The collection was started by Lionel de Rothschild, who personally made 1,210 crosses in his lifetime, 460 of which have been recognised by the

31

Royal Horitcultural Society and are in commercial cultivation.

Other connections of aristocratic families with Exbury and Lepe are evident in the church nearby. There are several memorials to the Mitford family and a private chapel donated by Henry Baron Forster, Governor-General of Australia during 1920-25. It is a memorial to the two sons he lost during the First World War: there is a full-size bronze effigy of one and a bronze relief of the other, both by the sculptor Cecil Thomas.

In a plot in the churchyard reserved for the de Rothschild family there are two simple tombstones.

Lower Exbury stands at the entrance to the Beaulieu river and gives a superb view of the islands and mudbanks which mark this part of the Solent. To the east are the remains of an old pier which served a local brickyard. A few small boats and yachts are moored here amidst the mudbanks, which are overgrown with sea purslane and alive with birds — geese, gulls, terns and many others.

A footpath to Lepe runs under the shore at this point, and trees grow down to the edge of the sea. It is a private shore where log groynes have been placed to minimise the constant nibbling of the sea: the low sandy cliffs where sand martins have their nests are vulnerable.

Hereabouts the sea bristles with the booms which mark the entrance channel of the Beaulieu river, which runs to the east for more than a mile before turning to the south and the open sea. On the beach at this point is a white-painted building that was for many years the coastguard station, ideally placed to have a close-up view of any vessel entering the river ! On the cliff above is a line of slate-hung cottages where the coastguards lived.

Further east is the estuary of the Dark Water, the small river that drains Beaulieu Heath. It now reaches the sea via a tunnel and sluice gate but in former times turned east to exit at Stone Point, on the site of the Lepe Country Park. This part of the coast has long been of importance as the closest point to the Isle of Wight (with the exception of Hurst, with its arduous shingle approach). It was the place from which Charles I left for Carisbrooke Castle and imprisonment and the traditional mustering point for militiamen bound for the Isle of Wight when the beacons were fired. Some authorities have suggested that there may have been a small Roman harbour in the vicinity, which would explain why an old road, which at one time was quite marked, ran from Stone Point across the northern edge of Beaulieu Heath to Dibden and beyond.

Lepe Country Park is an ideal picnic spot with superb views across to Isle of Wight from West Cowes to the Newtown estuary and further west. The coastal path continues for about two miles to the east, until it reaches the North Solent National Nature Reserve, which includes a shingle bank where such plants as yellow-horned poppy, viper's bugloss, sea-kale and little robin are preserved. For about a mile from this point there is no admittance to the shore.

At **Stansore Point** just to the east of the country park are two huge stanchions and, offshore, the remains of a jetty. These and the circular brick firefighting pond nearby are all connected with preparations for

Exbury Gardens

D-Day which were carried out here during the Second World War. Further east is an extensive concrete platform which marks the place where some of the large caissons called Phoenixes, part of the Mulberry harbours, were built and launched.

The 'missing link' in the coastal path between Lepe and Calshot belongs to the Drummond family, who have owned land in this part of Hampshire for more than 200 years. The first owner, Henry Drummond, was sent away from Scotland to escape the troubles of the '45 rising, made his fortune in the City and purchased agricultural land and mudlands on the west side of Southampton Water. Much of this land and the mansion house were on the site of what is now the Esso oil refinery.

The present family home, **Cadland House**, was built in 1934 on the site of a cottage ornée designed by Henry Holland in 1780 and burnt down in 1916. The genius of the architect's father-in-law, Capability Brown, can still be seen in the gardens which he landscaped, the smallest he ever worked on. The house is not open to the public.

If the walker wishes to travel from Lepe to Calshot he must take the back roads through the holdings of the Manor of Cadland to Hillhead, returning to the coast where a long line of beach huts stretches towards **Calshot Castle spit** and the Hampshire County Council Activities Centre.

To the west is a secluded shore under low sandy cliffs which can be walked for about a mile, until the limits of the North Solent National Nature Reserve prevent further progress. It was on this beach, historians have suggested, that the West Saxons first landed in 495 at the start of the conflict with the Britons that led to the kingdom of Wessex centred on Winchester as its capital.

Another point of interest is Luttrell's Tower, an intriguing 18th century folly which stands on the top of the cliff at the head of a flight of steps. It was here that Marconi carried out some of his first experimental transmissions to the Isle of Wight. The tower stands beside

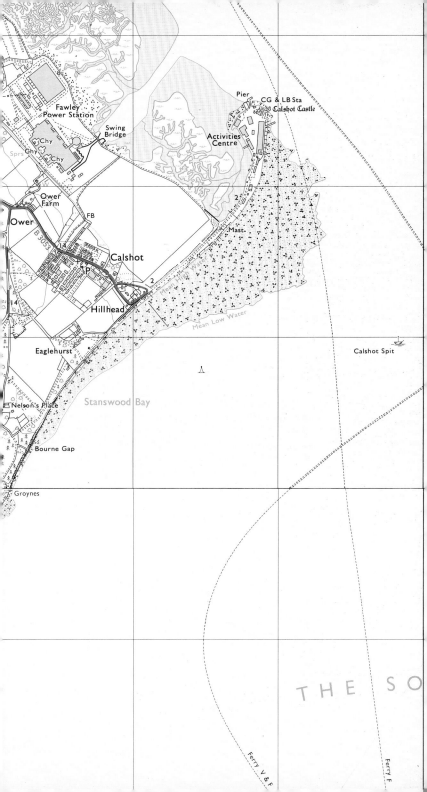

Fawley
Power Station

Swing
Bridge

Pier
CG & LB Sta
Calshot Castle

Activities
Centre

Chy
Ghy
Chy

Sprs

2

Ower
Farm

FB

Ower

Mast

B 3053

4

Calshot

P

2

4

Hillhead

Mean High Water

Mean Low Water

Eaglehurst

Calshot Spit

Stanswood Bay

Nelson's Place

Bourne Gap

Groynes

THE SO

Ferry V & F

Ferry F

Coast near Inchmery

Eaglehurst, a house which at one time was connected to Calshot spit by a narrow-gauge railway. At the time, the house served as a billet for Service personnel when in the First World War the Royal Flying Corps Naval Wing (later RNAS and then RAF) set up a seaplane station on the windswept peninsula alongside the Tudor castle and a coastguard station.

Calshot's association with seaplanes and flying boats continued for nearly forty years: it is now probably best remembered for being the home of the RAF High Speed Flight, which won the Schneider Trophy here in 1931. The old hangars have now been gaily decorated with huge dog-tooth patterns and are used by young people in a wide variety of activities, including sailing, canoeing and sports such as skiing and archery.

A footpath leads from Calshot village to Ashlett, where a former tide mill now serves as a social club. Nearby is the 600-foot stack of **Fawley** power station which is fed with oil by the Esso oil refinery to the north. This is the largest refinery in Britain and produces the full range of oil products, including of course petroleum. As mentioned above, it was built on land bought from the Drummond family. The first installation was set up by the Atlantic Gulf and West Indies Petroleum Company in 1921, but a dramatic fall in world prices soon created problems and caused the backers, Drummonds Bank, to call in overdrafts. After a series of takeovers the business became the property of the Standard Oil Company (New Jersey), now called the Exxon Corporation.

The modern refinery dates from the early 1950s, since when the site has continuously evolved to produce the complex of towers, tanks and chimneys which can now be seen. Fuel for the London market, including both Heathrow and Gatwick airports, is supplied by pipelines which run through a tunnel under Southampton Water to the west of the Hamble river.

BEAULIEU TO HYTHE

Palace House, Beaulieu

BEAULIEU TO HYTHE

Beaulieu was heralded with too much trumpeting and it undertook too much.

Dom F. Hockey, 1976

The Solent Way from Bucklers Hard emerges in **Beaulieu** at the back of the Montagu Arms. Across the river can be seen the great wall of the abbey precinct, the Palace House and the church, formerly the monks' refectory. Beyond that are the cloisters and further north the National Motor Museum and the vineyard.

The entire Beaulieu Manor Estate, which includes the villages of Bucklers Hard and Beaulieu and 20 farms and smallholdings, covers 8,000 acres, 2,000 of which are woodland.

Until the dissolution it was held by monks of the Cistercian order, but in 1538 it was bought for a song by Thomas Wriothesley, whose prime property was Place House, at Titchfield, between Southampton and Portsmouth.

The subsequent history of the Beaulieu site is reflected in its buildings. First there was the monastery. The ground plan of the huge abbey church has been laid out upon the ground alongside the cloisters. None of the building itself remains as its stone was used in the building of Hurst castle and other Solent defences.

The ruins of the cloisters, which contain a herb garden, were for some reason not destroyed. Along the west side run the lay brothers' frater and cellarium where an exhibition of monastic life has been set up.

We have already passed the grange at St Leonards, but that was only part of the elaborate fabric of monastic life at Beaulieu, the details of which have been preserved in an account book for a single year — from 29th September 1269 to 28th September 1270. This and other documents reveal the wealth of activity that went on at the abbey site itself. There was a mill, tannery, piggery, slaughter-house, brewery, fishmongers, forge, granary, bakehouse and stables !

The monastic system slowly decayed from its heyday, partly due to the shortage of cheap labour which it required. When Thomas Stevens, the abbot of Beaulieu, finally surrendered the abbey in April 1538 the community had been reduced to 21 men. Its demise was undoubtedly hastened by the vast numbers of 'felons and murderers' and their families who were able to claim sanctuary within its walls. And when the whole business was over, the abbot took a living at Bentworth, near Alton.

Neither Wriothesley nor any of the other early owners of Beaulieu took much interest in living there, though from time to time it was used as a country retreat or hunting lodge. The Palace House that can be seen now dates from the early 1870s, when the present owner's

Palace House

By the Beaulieu River

grandfather engaged the Victorian architect, Arthur Blomfield, to make a proper home of the former Great Gatehouse of the abbey. Its great vaulted ceilings and mock medieval fireplaces create the impression of a Scottish castle.

The next phase in Beaulieu's history is marked by the **National Motor Museum**, which was inspired by the great interest shown in transport by John 2nd Baron Montagu. Not only was he fascinated by the mechanics and design of the vehicles themselves but he also founded a magazine, *The Car Illustrated*, and conceived road systems that were close to present-day motorways. One of his plans, for overhead roads in London, might have dramatically changed traffic problems in the capital if it had been taken up.

The idea of a motor museum arose in the early 1950s, when Edward 3rd Baron Montagu first opened Beaulieu to the public. He placed a few old cars in the hall of the Palace House, then expanded with more cars in the old kitchens and also opened the world's first museum of motor cycles.

From these small beginnings has grown one of the largest collections of motor vehicles in the world, which since the early 1970s has been housed in a custom-built museum complex. This marks a new phase in Beaulieu's history; it is now a major tourist attraction. In addition to the museum, it has a monorail which circuits the grounds and actually passes through the museum, a 'Transporama' audiovisual presentation of the history of transport and many other entertainments for visitors.

The diversity of Beaulieu's activities begin to rival the workshops of the Cistercian monastery. To the north of the museum is a five-acre vineyard which was planted in the early 1960s. Depending on the season, it produces about 5-8,000 bottles of white and red wine, though its full potential is reckoned to be about 15,000 bottles. Vines were also grown by the monks, though there is no evidence that they ever made wine from them.

One of the most important episodes in Beaulieu's modern history is its role in the preparations for D-Day. Lower down at Exbury, HMS *Mastodon* was busily engaged in making landing craft ready (see p. 31), but Beaulieu and its outbuildings were equally involved. Eyewitnesses describe the area as being 'absolutely solid' with troops. Some of the houses on the estate were also used as training centres for Special Operations Executive personnel, who were later dropped in a number of European countries to work with local Resistance movements. And on the river the Royal Marines who were later dubbed 'The Cockleshell Heroes' practised some of the manoeuvres which later enabled them to destroy German ships anchored in the Gironde estuary in Bordeaux.

Ater Beaulieu the Solent Way climbs up to Hill Top and open heathland. But before setting out note the tidal mill on the river, beside the road to Hythe. It was in active use until 1927 and was briefly brought back into operation during the last war for the production of animal food.

Note also the main street of **Beaulieu village**, probably one of the best documented village centres in Hampshire. On the east side is The

Montagu Arms, so-called since 1742, though an inn under various names has probably been here since the 16th century. Like the New Inn at Bucklers Hard, it was both a centre of commerce and a hostelry until this century.

Moving further down the east side of Beaulieu Street, we come to 'Morris's' and 'Warners's', which stand on the site of an old hop garden. The other houses in the street have been occupied by the various tradesmen and craftsmen needed to sustain the estate and village community — tailor, maltster, shoemaker, grocer and many others.

At the south end of Beaulieu Street is 'The Lodge', built in about 1840 as a parsonage by Henry James Scott, Lord Montagu of Boughton, who wanted to be sure of attracting a vicar of the highest standing to the village. The church itself can be seen alongside the Solent Way on the way out of Beaulieu.

For nearly four centuries it was outside the jurisdiction of any bishop, a hangover from monastic days. Indeed, at least one incumbent adopted eccentric ways based on the notion that he was imbued with the authority of the former abbot and that he was 'in continuous touch with the monks'.

One of the most interesting features of the church is the rare example of a monastic lector's pulpit, which is approached by a flight of steps built into the wall of the old monks' refectory. The church is also rich in memorials.

The trail now continues to **Hill Top.** On the south side of the climb out of Beaulieu is the Out of Town Centre, formerly the Home Farm, where city children come into contact with farm life and the countryside under the guidance of TV personality Jack Hargreaves.

Further up the hill, in private woodland a short distance from the north side of the Hythe road, is the Monks Well. In an area which is never short of groundwater, the trouble taken by the Cistercians to channel the waters of this ancient spring to Beaulieu is testimony to their appreciation of the dangers of waterborne infection. The tomb-like well-head, dark and mysterious, is now in a poor state of repair, but after the waters were repiped to Beaulieu in the 1830s it continued to be used until recent times.

Hill Top is a thin straggling settlement just beyond the boundary of the Beaulieu Manor Estate and on the edge of open heathland grazed by New Forest ponies. Its position and its form come from its origins as a squatters' village: here men were free to build their own houses (tradition says it had to be done in a single night) and claim Commoners' Rights and yet they were close to Beaulieu. None of the original squatters' cottages remains at Hill Top, though contemporary descriptions suggest they were rough-and-ready timber structures with cob walls.

Beyond Hill Top is **Beaulieu Heath**, a barren expanse of moor and gorse. It has been planted with forest towards Hythe, but apart from a few gorse-covered tumuli and the line of a Roman road to Lepe it appears quite featureless.

This was certainly the view of William Cobbett, the outspoken author of *Rural Rides*. Crossing from Beaulieu to Marchwood in 1826

Beaulieu Heath, Hill Top

he called it an 'intolerable heath' and went on to say: 'Never was a more barren tract of land than these seven or eight miles.'

But there is another way to view Beaulieu Heath, best expressed by that author-naturalist W.H. Hudson. In his *Hampshire Days* he first of all points out that the heath is not as flat as it looks, 'it is grooved with long valley-like depressions with marshy or boggy bottoms . . .'. Then he describes the vegetation ('One may wade through acres of myrtle, until the subtle delightful odour is in one's skin and clothes . . .') and the birdlife — the nesting nightjar, snipe and redshank. And he watches a spider catch and paralyse an unfortunate grasshopper.

Hudson also captures another feature of the heath, its atmosphere of mysticism. He describes how he sat on one of the barrows until the sun had set, 'held by the silence and solitariness of that mound of the ancient dead . . .'.

Today, Hudson's mood might be affected by the huge stack of the oil-fired power station at Fawley and the smaller chimneys of the Esso oil refinery that can be seen across the heath. Further north are the twin stacks of another power station at Marchwood. These marks of the industry on the western side of Southampton Water, known locally as The Waterside, have been visible since the trail left Sowley Pond. At Hythe a close-up view of some of the pipes and tanks which sustain a modern chemical works can be seen at the Esso Hythe Terminal, where road tankers come and go.

The Solent Way runs alongside electricity pylons for a mile or so and then takes an ingenious route to the centre of **Hythe**, down an old twisting lane, Hart Hill. It leads to the huge drowned estuary that has dictated the fortunes of the area, Southampton Water. The view of the shore stretches from the cranes of the Eastern Docks and the Itchen Bridge at Southampton to the BP oil terminal at Hamble.

In between are the sheds of Vosper Thornycroft, the shipbuilders, at Woolston, with Weston's tower blocks to the south-east, then Netley Castle and the green-domed chapel of the former Royal Victoria Hospital at Netley. It is a wooded shore which tapers off beyond Hamble, towards Hill Head and Lee-on-Solent. On this side are the flares and lights of the Esso oil refinery.

The Hythe foreshore gives a grandstand view of the traffic of boats in Southampton Water: the cutters of the docks authorities and the Police; ferries and hydrofoil between Southampton and Cowes; containerships and the occasional liner; and, towards Fawley, the huge oil tankers which bring crude stocks from the Middle East for distillation and processing.

Many of the people who work in the local refinery and chemical works live at Hythe, but it is also a dormitory suburb for Southampton. Commuters make the daily journey across the water in the *New Forester*, a modern ferry with plush seats and a panoramic view of the dockside.

The path of the Solent Way to the centre of the town passes some rather dull-looking sheds with an interesting past. They belong to the Ministry of Defence and are covered by the provisions of the Official Secrets Act. Behind them and some way offshore is a long line of grey-painted barges. We cannot enquire what happens in this area now, but in the past these great sheds were used for maintenance by BOAC and their predecessors in business, Imperial Airways and Supermarine Aviation. The 'airfield' was Southampton Water and the aircraft were flying boats.

Commercial flying in the area was started in 1919 by Hubert Scott-Paine, the owner of the Supermarine Aviation Works at Woolston. The heyday of the flying boats was in the 'thirties and 'forties, when Imperial Airways and BOAC operated Empire class aircraft. In 1937 the first proving flight was made from Hythe across the Atlantic to Newfoundland. In these early days of air travel the fastest crossing took 10½ hours. Routes were quickly extended to the centres of the British Empire — to Karachi, Hong Kong and Singapore.

After the war, BOAC operated from Southampton and Poole, though all aircraft were maintained at Hythe. A fleet of Sunderland flying boats, which were used by BOAC in the early 'forties, were christened Hythes.

A new BOAC air terminal was opened in Southampton's Eastern Docks in 1948, but within a year the company announced that no more flying boats would be operated. The age of the land plane had come, hastened by the large number of airstrips built during the war.

Hythe was also the home of the British Power Boat Company, which built high-speed craft. Founded by Hubert Scott-Paine, mentioned above, the company built the first single-engined boat to reach 100 mph, the *Miss Britain III*, which can be seen in the Maritime Museum at Southampton. Many other craft were built at Hythe, including Motor Torpedo Boats and high-speed launches for the RAF. Aircraftsman T. E. Shaw, better known as Lawrence of Arabia, was one of the Service officers to work on the boats.

'Queen Elizabeth II' from the Hythe Ferry

After Hythe the Solent Way crosses by ferry to **Southampton**. The pier from which the boat leaves is one of the delights of the town. More than two thousand feet long, it dates from 1880. Since 1922 it has been traversed by a narrow gauge railway which makes the trip to the end of the pier an experience rather like a ride at the fair.

The crossing to Southampton is a chance to untangle the geography of the docks and the upper reaches of Southampton Water. To the far left are the chimneys of Marchwood power station and further up, on the opposite shore, the Prince Charles Container terminal standing on reclaimed land. Below this are the Western Docks, a single quay nearly a mile and a half long lined with cranes. The ferry makes for the Eastern Docks, the oldest part of the complex, dating from Victorian times. The first part to be reached is the Queen Elizabeth II Terminal, on the right, alongside the tower of the Port Signal and Radar Station. Here the *QE2* docks and further on is the Ocean Dock, where the *Queen Mary* and *Queen Elizabeth* used to tie up.

The ferry comes in alongside the Town Quay. Immediately ahead is a distinctive domed building which used to be the offices of the Southampton Harbour Board before nationalisation, and most recently privatisation of the docks. Across the road is a fragment of the medieval town wall. It is a telling symbol of Southampton, a city with a visible history that is little known outside the area.

Bugle Street

SOUTHAMPTON

*The town is handsome, and for the bigness of it as fair houses
as be at London.*

Edward VI, 1552

When common sense says that the tide ought to be turning at
Southampton it will 'hang about' for an hour or two more.
This so-called 'double high tide', which enables ships to come
and go more readily, is one of the major benefits of Southampton as a
port. It is produced by complex oscillations of water within the English
Channel and between the Isle of Wight and the Cherbourg peninsula.
And the fact that the tidal stream can reach Southampton from both
ends of the Solent produces other tidal effects.

Another major advantage of the port is its natural deep water, which
J.B. Priestley has called 'so many fathoms of luck'. Also its general
position, relatively close to London, and facing the French coast has
given Southampton a natural importance for many centuries.

In recent years archaeological excavations to the east of the modern
dockside have revealed the remains of a very substantial town called
Hamwih on the west bank of the Itchen. Founded in AD 700, it is
thought to have been the largest town in England at the time with a population of about 9,000. Further upstream on the opposite bank is the
site of a Roman port, **Clausentum**, now built over by the modern suburb of Bitterne.

In the middle ages the town moved to the present dockside area,
where a great deal of the old wall can still be seen. At this time
Southampton thrived as an entrepôt that exported English wool and
imported wines and other goods. To the north-west of the Town Quay
on the landward side of the road is the **Wool House**, an imposing
medieval building which now houses the Maritime Museum. Several
other medieval buildings survive and below ground level are a number
of the vaults which were used for storage.

The Maritime Museum tells the story of Southampton's dockside
and the ships that used it. Just inside the Wool House is a huge model of
the docks, built in 1938 by Southern Railway, then the owners, for the
New York World Fair. There are also engines from old steamers and
ship models in the museum, including one of the *Queen Mary* 22ft in
length. Note also the exhibit on the Ocean Terminal, a luxury facility
for liner passengers which was opened in 1950. Alas, Southampton's
liner traffic was soon to fall away as more and more people travelled by
air and the terminal was recently demolished.

The Maritime Museum also has a display on the *Titanic*, the ill-fated
liner that sailed from Southampton in 1912, and an extensive exhibit on
the British Power Boat Company of Hythe and the work of Hubert
Scott-Paine.

Landing craft in Southampton Docks before D-Day

To the west of the Wool House is the **Mayflower Monument**, a needle-shaped memorial which records the fact that the Pilgrim Fathers, religious dissenters from Nottinghamshire, set sail from Southampton for the New World in the *Mayflower* and *Speedwell* in 1620. They departed from the West Quay close to the site of the memorial, but had to leave the *Speedwell* at Plymouth because she was unseaworthy.

Note also on the Mayflower Monument a number of other plaques, including one to mark the two million men and women who left Southampton between D-Day, 6th June 1944, and the liberation of Europe. Southampton and its hinterland was a major focus of troop concentrations prior to embarkation. Harbours and inlets all round the Solent were involved in the preparations and large parts of the Mulberry harbours which were set up on the beaches of Normandy were built and assembled in Southampton Docks.

When the flotilla of ships and landing craft left the Solent it looked, as an eyewitness wrote later, 'for all the world as though one could walk to the Isle of Wight without getting one's feet wet'. But it was hardly a new role for the town. Almost every national conflict, from Crécy onwards, has involved major military embarkations of men and equipment from Southampton. The feelings of at least one man, Thomas Hardy, have been recorded. In October 1899 at the start of the Boer War, during which half a million men were to leave Southampton, he asked:

When shall saner softer polities
Whereof we dream have sway . . .?

Opposite the Mayflower Monument is Mayflower Park, which is brought alive each autumn by the Southampton International Boat

'Queen Elizabeth I' in Southampton Docks

Southampton Bargate, early 19th C.

Show. From its beginnings in 1969 it has grown to be an annual event which rivals the London Boat Show.

Between the monument and the West Gate of the medieval wall are preserved several dwellings which became incorporated in the structure. At one time they would have looked out on to open water, for the whole area under the wall, between Western Esplanade (note the name) and the sea, was reclaimed during the building of the Western Docks in the late 1920s. When Jane Austen lived in Southampton and 'took the airs' she would have looked out over a shallow, gently curving bay that is now given over to the dockside.

The **West Gate** led to Southampton's main medieval quay, from which Henry V embarked for Agincourt. Alongside the West Gate is a Tudor merchant's hall which was used for storing wool. You are now in a part of the city which is remarkably little known by modern visitors, though it is crammed with rare sights. Turn left into Bugle Street and ahead you will find a 15th century house built by John Dawtry, Controller of the King's Customs, now the Tudor House Museum. Although much modified over the ages, the house is a grand building which exudes all the confidence of a successful Tudor burgess.

The **Tudor House Museum** has a superb display of local treasures, including a statuette and portrait of Charles Dibdin, a Southampton man who came to be known as the 'sailor's poet'. Many of the patriotic songs which he wrote, of which the best known was probably *Tom Bowling*, were played on the spinet which stands alongside his portrait.

Note also the collection of Sunderland Ware, a form of gift china which was traded between ports by sailors as a sideline.

The museum also has a fine picture of the High Street, Southampton, painted in 1808 by Tobias Young. It is a reminder that Southampton was a fashionable spa town until Regency times, when its fortunes as a port were at a low ebb.

Behind the museum is a reconstruction of a Tudor town garden which contains more than a hundred plants and herbs typical of the period. It is decorated with authentic striped rails and posts topped with heraldic beasts and has a 'secret garden' with bees in a straw skep.

Beyond the garden is a very rare sight, a Norman house, dating from 1150-75 and sometimes called King John's House. A Norman fireplace and chimney, re-erected from elsewhere in the city, can be seen, together with the earliest known examples of gunports, which were inserted in the wall in about 1360. Before modern reclamation, the gunports looked out on the sea and were intended as defence against surprise attacks, like the French raid of 1338, which ruined the town for many years.

Opposite the Tudor House Museum is **St. Michael's Church** which was built shortly after the Conquest. Inside are four huge arches from the original structure which support the tower of the church. There are a number of treasures, including a carved black marble font which was brought from Tournai in Belgium in the 12th century and two medieval brass lecterns. The tomb of Sir Richard Lyster, sometime Henry VIII's Chief Justice of England, who married Sir John Dawtry's widow and lived at the Tudor House, is just inside the church. The fine octagonal spire of the church dates from 1732.

The walker may here decide to take a short cut back towards the dockside (skip to the asterisk - p. 55) or a circuitous path which takes in some of the finest medieval walls to be seen anywhere. If you choose the longer route, continue up Bugle Street, alongside the modern mews development, Postern Court and Biddles Gate Court, to Simnel Street. On the north-east corner of this junction is the **Undercroft,** a fine early 14th century stone building which was the ground floor of a medieval house, probably built in timber.

Turning left into a path opposite Simnel Street and right along Western Esplanade, you come to a long section of the old city wall which runs up to the splendid battlements of Catchcold Tower and Arundel Tower, past the site of the castle. A staircase called Forty Steps leads up the side of the wall to a walk along the ramparts.

Perhaps the finest preserved feature of the medieval city wall is the **Bargate**, the oldest building in use in the city. Much of the structure is the original Norman gateway dating from 1175-1200. The stern north side was remodelled in the 14th century and machiolations were added to make it easier 'to drop things' on assailants. The leaden lions represent the beasts who featured in that popular medieval romance in which Southampton's legendary hero, Sir Bevis of Hampton, is careful to establish the purity of his loved one before marriage. Panels which once flanked the lions, showing scenes from the story, can be seen in the museum which is housed at the top of the Bargate in the former Guildhall.

Modern Southampton has developed around the shopping street called Above Bar, but south of the Bargate is the original **High Street**. This thoroughfare was formerly called English Street to mark the English quarter of the medieval city. To the west is French Street where the Norman merchants settled after the Conquest.

High Street has three old inns, all on the east side. First comes The Star Hotel, a Georgian inn built around an earlier medieval house, which retains the arched entrance through which coaches passed in and out and an old coaching sign. Below is The Dolphin Hotel, with splendid Georgian bow windows that were built at a time when grand balls were held in the Winter Assembly Rooms on the first floor of the inn.

Across the High Street from St. Michael's church are the ruins of Holy Rood church, badly damaged by German bombs in 1940, when the centre of Southampton was devastated. (Incidently, about the only benefit of the blitz was that it revealed a number of medieval vaults.) The church is now dedicated to the men of the Merchant Navy who have been lost at sea, and includes memorials to the 'stewards, sailors and firemen' who went down with the *Titanic* and those killed in the Falkland Islands campaign.

South of the church is The Red Lion Inn which is traditionally the place where the conspirators who plotted against Henry V in 1415, just as he was leaving for Agincourt, were tried and condemned to death. They were beheaded just north of the Bargate, and the tradition is marked at the inn by the name of a fine hall, the Court Room.

At the foot of High Street are the ruins of Water Gate Tower in Porters Lane, which also contains the remains of a Norman house, erroneously called **Canute's Palace**, after the Danish king who is reputed to have rebuked his courtiers and failed to stem the advancing tide at Southampton.

Opposite is Winkle Street, which leads past **God's House Hospital**, to the gatehouse and tower which also bear the name of this 12th century hospice. A museum of archaeology in God's House Tower shows some of the fine medieval French pottery found in Southampton and also includes displays on Roman Clausentum and Saxon Hamwih, important settlements on the Itchen.

From the bottom of High Street the walker's most direct route out of town is along Platform Road, beyond which lie the Eastern Docks. Look out for a plaque in Vosper Shiprepairers' yard, which records the site of the original foundation stone which was laid in 1838 and marked the start of a custom-built docks system.

* The shortest cut from St. Michael's church is not without interest — for across the High Street are the ruins of Holy Rood and beyond this a turning to the right off Bernard Street is the cul-de-sac Oxford Street. This once fashionable shopping street leads down to the town's first railway terminus built in 1840. It was abandoned in 1966 with the disappearance of the Atlantic liner passengers. The grand former railway hotel which dwarfs the handsome station also lost its custom and now houses the local BBC radio station. In the last war its many rooms were also used for office space in the months before and after D Day, when it

Southampton Hall of Aviation

was taken over as the headquarters for military movement control.

Canute Road leads to the **Itchen Bridge**, opened in 1977, which replaced a floating bridge that plied across the water to Woolston. At the foot of the bridge on the dockside shore is the **Southampton Hall of Aviation**, which incorporates the Mitchell Museum and tells the story of the development of the aircraft industry in the Solent area. Dedicated to the memory of R. J. Mitchell, the designer who created the Spitfire, the museum was built around a full-size Sandringham flying boat which dominates the exhibits. It also includes a Spitfire and the Supermarine S6A machine which won the 1929 Schneider race for Britain, prior to the outright winning of the trophy two years later.

The Itchen Bridge provides a grandstand view of the working river. On the Woolston side to the south are the yards of Vosper Thornycroft, where naval vessels are constructed on a site which has been used by shipbuilders for more than a century. There is a clear view of the Esso oil refinery and on the Southampton shore is Princess Alexandra Dock, where several berths for roll on-roll off traffic are located.

Upstream on the east bank is Peartree Green and above that the works of Vosper Hovermarine. Opposite are the old wharfs leading up to Northam, where the well-known shipbuilders, Day, Summers built mail steamers and luxury steam yachts.

WOOLSTON
TO
HAMBLE

Netley Abbey Ruins

WOOLSTON TO HAMBLE

I saw thee, Netley, as the sun
Across the western wave
Was sinking low. And a golden glow
To thy roofless towers he gave.

The Ingoldsby Legends, 1840

Woolston is famous for aircraft and ships. The Supermarine Aviation Company was set up on the present site of Vosper Hovermarine, whilst ships were built downstream where Vosper Thornycroft now produce naval frigates and mine counter-measure vessels in glass reinforced plastic. (Incidently, the two companies are separately owned.)

Most of the Supermarine factory was blitzed during the last war but some parts of its still remain. Aircraft were first built on the Itchen by Noel Pemberton-Billing, an early entrepreneur in the business who set up a factory at Woolston in 1913. Pemberton-Billing was a colourful enthusiast. In 1903 he built a man-lifting kite and when flying machines were invented he managed to become a 'certified aviator' after only three hours' training.

Much of the managerial skill which later made Supermarine famous came, however, from Hubert Scott-Paine, the owner who used the design genius of R. J. Mitchell to capture the Schneider Trophy in 1931 and then go on to create the Spitfire.

Scott-Paine not only built aircraft at Woolston but he also operated them. In 1919 he started a regular service between Woolston and three local destinations — Southsea, Bournemouth and the Isle of Wight — flying Supermarine Channel flying boats. For a short while he also flew between Southampton and Le Havre, the first international service to be operated in Britain.

Later, in 1923, in a joint venture with Southern Railway, who at that time owned the docks at Southampton, he set up regular flights between Woolston and the Channel Islands. This quickly led to the formation of Imperial Airways, which continued to fly from Woolston as its 'airport' until about 1930, and ten years later became part of BOAC.

During the last war part of the blitzed Supermarine factory was pressed into use by HMS *Abatos*, the naval establishment that carried out trials of PLUTO (PipeLine Under The Ocean) and later laid the lines that were to provide some of the essential petroleum needed to keep up the momentum of the Allied invasion of France in 1944. Flexible lead-walled piping (in effect, submarine cable without the copper core) was laid across the Channel from pumping stations on the Isle of Wight to Cherbourg by cable-laying ships manned by *Abatos* personnel. Steel pipelines were also laid by vessels that looked like huge cotton reels

The Solent Way near Weston

and carried 70 miles of welded 3″ tubing.

The Solent Way through Woolston passes the works of **Vosper Thornycroft**, where naval frigates and other vessels are often to be seen. Shipbuilding on this site was started in 1876 by Thomas Oswald, a Sunderland man. Though he succeeded in building vessels up to 5,000 tons, the yard involved so many accidents that it was called 'the slaughterhouse' by his workers. Later the yard was taken over by John (later Sir John) Thornycroft, the famous shipbuilder who came to Woolston from Chiswick in 1904. He laid the foundations of a firm which became internationally renowned for its naval ships, a tradition which continues.

Shortly after the trail returns to the sea, at the entrance to the Itchen river, it passes the longest building in Hampshire, a huge brick edifice 2,000 feet in length. But despite its immense size, its original function is rather obscure. It was probably built as a rolling mill but the First World War intervened and it became instead a munitions metal-working factory. Its continuous production lines were amongst the most advanced in the world and included a foundry, rolling mills, a cupping works (for drawing up shell cases from solid brass) and a laboratory. And the entire factory was so large that it had its own coal-fired power station and gas-producing plant.

Since Armistice Day, 1918, when the factory was promptly shut down, this substantial building has had a chequered career, with no one quite able to find the ideal use for half a mile of sturdy brickwork. Since the last war it has been used as a Naval store.

Beyond the store is **Weston**, a suburb of Southampton which is probably best known for the five identical tower blocks which act as a prominent landmark around the Solent. It also happens to be one of those places enshrined in English literature, because William Cobbett stayed at Weston Grove, the mansion house of the local landowner, Thomas Chamberlayne, and wrote about the experience in *Rural Rides*. And it is very, very complimentary. He says: 'To those who like water scenes (as nineteen-twentieths of people do) it is the prettiest spot, I believe, in all England.'

As you walk the shore today you are right to wonder whether Cobbett was writing about another place. The answer to the riddle is given as you approach Netley, where woodland spreads across the road to the edge of the sea. Now imagine woods like these stretching back to Woolston and a shoreline as undeveloped as that beside the Beaulieu river and you have some idea of what Cobbett saw. Probably the only mark on the beach was a crude hut bedecked with seaweed at the bottom of what is now Weston Lane, where a pub's name is a reminder of this shelter for local fishermen and their nets.

The city of Southampton extends for about another mile, where a small stream runs into the sea from Weston Park. Just beyond this point the Solent Way passes **Netley Castle**, a Tudor-style mansion which mainly dates from the 1880s, when it was remodelled and its baronial interiors — including huge stone fireplaces and wood panelling — were put in by its new owner, Colonel Sir Harry Crichton. The imposing stone edifice, which has been a convalescent home since the last war, is on the site of a fort which was built at about the time of Hurst and Calshot castles. Like St Andrews castle at Hamble, of which little remains, it was later reckoned to be an unnecessary defence work and was only garrisoned until 1627. With the possible exception of the archway in the main entrance, none of the original Tudor fort remains.

Just above the castle stand the ruins of **Netley Abbey**, beloved by Victorians for its picturesqueness. In fact, the trees and ivy which flourished at this time threatened to destroy the buildings. The Department of the Environment now maintains the ruins, a substantial part of which still remains, notably the south transept and chapter house and the fine east window of the presbytery. In the north-east corner of the south transept is a spiral staircase which may have led to the tower where the monks of the Cistercian monastery maintained a navigation light for mariners. Certainly when the commissioners reported on Netley and the handful of monks left at the dissolution in 1536 they remarked specifically that the abbey was 'To the Kinges Subjects and Strangers travelinge the same Sees great reliefe and Comforte'.

Another interesting feature worth looking for is the 'four-seater' rere-dorter or lavatory which, like many more modern sewage schemes, was flushed straight into Southampton Water.

Netley abbey was established as a daughter-house of Beaulieu at the instigation of Peter des Roches, bishop of Winchester. It was, however, formally founded and dedicated to St Edward the Confessor by Henry III in 1239 after the bishop's death, though it received no endowments until 13 years later. Memorials of the foundation, cut into

Royal Victoria Country Park

the bases of the piers of the transept crossing, can still be seen.

The history of the abbey is poorly documented, possibly because any surviving records went up in flames during the Civil War when Basing House, near Basingstoke, was destroyed. This was the home of the 5th Marquis of Winchester, whose ancestor, Sir William Paulet, was granted Netley's lands and buildings at the dissolution. Sir William's policy of bending his religious views to the sovereign of the time enabled him to live to an old age but attracted the contempt of Cobbett, who called him 'the most famous in the whole world for sycophancy, time-serving, and for all those qualities which usually distinguish the favourites of kings like the wife-killer', meaning of course Henry VIII.

When Sir William took over Netley abbey he is reputed to have used the nave of the church as a tennis court, stabled horses in the refectory and had dinner cooked in the chapter house.

The abbey was sold in the 18th century for building material to a local man, Walter Taylor, who was severely injured by falling masonry during demolition and subsequently died at the hands of a surgeon. The moral flavour of the tale is improved by the tradition that he was forewarned of the event in a dream, and even sought the advice of such men as Isaac Watts the Southampton hymn-writer, but greed got the better of him!

Close by the abbey is a classic example of Victorian copybook architecture, the church of St Edward the Confessor, built in 1886 by J.R. Sedding, the same architect who modernised the castle.

Beyond the abbey and the castle is the **Royal Victoria Country Park**, a 220-acre site with avenues of Scots pine which looks out over Southampton Water. In the centre is a green-domed chapel which is all

that remains of the huge military hospital where in *A Study in Scarlet* Conan Doyle chose to train Dr Watson as a surgeon before sending him off to be severely wounded in the Second Afghan War of 1878-79. In reality, most of the many thousands who came to Netley were injured before their visit. They came from all the theatres of colonial war and for many years were ferried from troopships to the 570-foot-long pier which ran out from the hospital, the foot of which is still clearly visible on the sea-wall opposite the chapel. Later the hospital was provided with its own railway station for the patients who landed in Southampton docks.

The few traces of this great building that remain give little idea of the grandeur of its scale. It was in fact 1,404 feet in length, had a thousand beds and cost £350,000 when it was built in 1856-63. Its huge facade dominated Southampton Water and was thought by some to be quite out of place. John Wise, the historian of the New Forest, for example, took a sideswipe at it when it was brand-new, saying 'the new Government Hospital loads the shore with all its costly ugliness'. Photographs of the Royal Victoria show that he was less than fair; but the building looked more like a grand barracks than a hospital. And it would have sat more comfortably alongside the Thames.

Much more important than Wise's criticism was the view of Florence Nightingale, who in the Crimean War had laboured to improve the medical care of the sick and the wounded. She did not approve of the design of the Royal Victoria Hospital. She criticised it for putting the wards on the northern side of the building, for providing insufficient windows and, above all, for having corridors a quarter of a mile long which might be 'a permanent receptacle for contaminated effluvia'. The Prime Minister at the time, Lord Palmerston, who lived near her in Romsey, accepted her arguments, but nonetheless the building went ahead. There was little that could be done to counter its principal supporter, Queen Victoria.

Although many patients were later said to find the place depressing, none of Florence Nightingale's arguments seems to have been substantiated by events. Nor were fears of Netley's proneness to infectious disease suggested by others ever proven. True, a severe outbreak of fever (for which, incidently, the prescription was a bottle of porter) had taken place when men were encamped at Netley during the Napoleonic Wars. But local enquiries showed that fisherfolk who lived on mudbound hulks offshore were perfectly healthy.

The Royal Victoria Hospital was built in great haste as a sort of reflex reaction to the horrors of the Crimean War, when 18,000 of the 54,000 British troops sent out to fight died and another 9,000 were made invalid. Although the Treasury resisted attempts to have proper medical facilities built, the cause was eventually won when Queen Victoria and Prince Albert lent their support. Within three months of the end of the war, the Queen was stepping ashore at Netley to lay the foundation stone. Underneath she placed a copper box containing coins, a Crimean medal and the first Victoria Cross, which were all recovered when the hospital was demolished in 1966.

On completion of the hospital in 1863 the Army Medical School moved there from Chatham, where it had been set up a few years before. Many medical advances were worked out at Netley, including improvements in treating gunshot wounds and better methods of public sanitation. One of the most famous doctors to work at the hospital was probably Sir Almroth Wright, who discovered an anti-typhoid vaccine here. Unfortunately it was not available in time to be used during the Boer War, when 15,000 men died from typhus and many others came to Netley to be nursed. One outcome of an enquiry held after the war was to transfer the Army Medical School to London, where it could benefit from contacts with other medical research establishments.

During both the Boer War and the First World War the No. 1 British Red Cross Hospital was located at Netley in an encampment to the north. To the east of the main hospital site is a cemetery with 700 graves, representing just a few of the men who died at Netley during 1914-18. On the banks of a stream nearby the Indian dead were cremated in the belief that their spirit would be transported back to the sacred Ganges.

The Royal Victoria Hospital continued to be used during the last war, when many of the victims of Dunkirk and D-Day were nursed at Netley. During the latter years of the war the hospital was taken over by the Americans, who are said to have found the corridors so long that they drove jeeps up and down them.

The Solent Way continues towards the Hamble river, past the works of **British Aerospace**, where aircraft components are manufactured. Like Calshot, Hythe and Woolston, this is another important site in the history of British aviation, for during the First World War Sir Alliott Verdon-Roe, the first Englishman to fly, set up a model factory here to build seaplanes for the Royal Naval Air Service. At a rate of seven per week, Avro 504 aircraft were built and launched into Southampton Water. There is a fine memorial to 'AV', as Sir Alliott was known, in St Andrew's church, Hamble.

Beyond **Westfield Common** the trail passes under the jetty of the Hamble Terminal, owned by BP Oil Ltd and used also by Shell UK Oil: in the parlance of the oil industry, it is a 'wet' installation for BP and a 'dry' one for Shell. Opened in 1924 as a fuel oil bunkering service for ships, the facility now stores a wide variety of petroleum products in 67 tanks with a total capacity of 250,000 tonnes. Note that the jetty leaves headroom at the landward end: this is said to have been provided so that local people could continue to cart seaweed from the shore for use as fertiliser.

Ahead are the masts and rigging of yachts in the Fairey marina: it is a foretaste of a Solent river where sailors and their craft cluster like bees on a honeycomb.

HAMBLE
TO
TITCHFIELD

The Hamble River

HAMBLE TO TITCHFIELD

Yachting every day of the week
Every day bar Sunday —
We finishes up of a Saturday night
And starts again on Monday.

Traditional

In yachting circles throughout the world the **Hamble River** is famous. More boats and more clubs are found here than in any other comparable inlet. And yet its popularity is a relatively new phenomenon which gathered pace after the last war and has now reached cult status. In addition to the many moorings and yards on the Hamble where boats are kept, there are now four large marinas on the river, including Port Hamble, the first marina ever to be built in Britain. But what is special about the Hamble? What is it that has made it such a popular haven with boat owners?

It is tempting to say 'lots of facilities' — but this begs the question. The real answer is that it has good deep water at all states of the tide, is conveniently situated and well sheltered. And these virtues have favoured it for centuries: writing in the early 8th century about the double tides of the Solent area, Bede chose to guide his readers to the right part of the country by referring to the Hamble. It is even said that the closeness of the river to Portsmouth helped the Tudors to decide to base a dockyard there, since the Hamble had been an ideal place for laying up naval vessels from Southampton.

Merchant and naval ships are now too large for the Hamble, but until the early 19th century large wooden ships were built at **Bursledon** up river and at Warsash on the opposite bank. The heyday of this business was at Bursledon in the late 17th and 18th centuries when many Admiralty contracts were placed here and at Bucklers Hard (see p. 27). The streets of Hamble village still echo these days: note Copperhill Terrace and Ropewalk, names which recall locally made rope and the copper vessels in which tar was heated.

The place of the Hamble as a working river really declined in the 1890s, when local fishermen found it much more amenable to crew for wealthy yacht owners at Cowes and elsewhere during the summer months than toil at their nets and dredges. They sailed round the coast of Britain, as far afield as the Clyde, racing their owner's craft in the most important regattas of the day.

At this time the Hamble was also used by the T.S. *Mercury*, an old hulk used as a training ship for poor young boys who wanted to go to sea. Started on the Isle of Wight in 1885 by the banker, Charles Hoare, *Mercury* continued after his death under the direction of C.B. Fry, the scholar and athlete. His friendship with Baden-Powell led in 1910 to the establishment on board *Mercury*, of the first Sea Scout troop in the

Hamble, and the Ferry shelter, Warsash.

country. Until a shortage of funds closed down the ship in 1968, the boys of *Mercury* were a familiar sight on the river.

As yachting on the river grew, a number of important clubs took premises in the area. The very first was a small branch of the Minima Sailing Club, which had a clubhouse built at the entrance to the river in 1891. But a sure sign that yachting had come to the river in a big way was when the Royal Southern Yacht Club moved in 1936 from impressive premises alongside the Wool House in Southampton to four cottages on the quay at Hamble. This famous haunt of ocean-going yachtsmen, including former Prime Minister Mr Edward Heath, is still there, at the foot of the winding main street of the village.

The hard at Hamble (which, incidently, was built up by American servicemen using the rubble of a blitzed Southampton) is a good vantage point from which to survey the lower reaches of the river. Upstream on this side is Port Hamble marina and boatyard. Downstream is the Hamble River Sailing Club, renowned for providing Olympic yachtsmen, and beyond the (by now) familiar spit at the river entrance, where there is another large marina. On the opposite shore is Warsash and the black and white tower of the harbour master, the steward of the river.

The Solent Way now takes its third ferry, across the river in a small motor boat based on the Hamble side. There is no schedule but the ferry runs without fail on request, and has done so for at least 500 years. On the **Warsash** side is a small concrete shelter which bears the name of Wm. Cooper & Co., brewers, who bought the ancient rights to the ferry from Winchester College in the early 1900s. The same company also owned a pub in the village called The Ferry House, later renamed The Bugle. It was probably here that the young solicitor in Nevile Shute's

What Happened to the Corbetts, written before the war, caught up on news of the blitz in Southampton which had forced him and his family to live aboard their boat on the Hamble.

One of the charms of the Hamble ferry is its casualness. Before it was driven by motor, passengers would often ease the ferryman's lot by taking a turn at the oars. And one ferryman used to ask passengers if they would mind pulling the boat ashore as he had a leak in his waders!

The boatmen here and at Eastney opposite Hayling Island are, by the way, the last men on the Solent who carry on what used to be an important trade; the wherryman. At Hythe and Gosport, for example, men used to line the approach to the shore to seek the traveller's custom.

Occasionally the Hamble ferry strikes gold. It happened in 1971 when more than 1,500 passengers took the crossing on the day that Chay Blyth returned to the river after completing his epic circumnavigation of the world.

The ferry touches land on the Warsash shore at the halfway point of the Solent Way. A recently restored footpath leads along the east bank of the river amongst the saltings and mud-banks up towards Swanwick and the Bursledon bridge. A path on the west bank continues up to Botley through the attractive Upper Hamble Country Park.

On the Warsash shore you might catch sight of the pennant of the local sailing club — a black lobster on a yellow background. This gives a clue to the lobster and crab teas for which the Hamble was once famous. The carriages and cars of the well-to-do from Southampton and elsewhere were once a familiar sight in Shore Road, and the trade did not die out until well after the Second World War. The crabs and lobsters were bought from local fishermen in the West Country, Brittany and Southern Ireland and transported to the Hamble in specially constructed boats. At Warsash they were stored in large ponds and then taken by rail to London and other large cities.

The river was also once famous for its oysters, 20,000 of which were sent each year at Lent to St Swithun's, Winchester, by the monks of the Benedictine Priory of St Andrew, Hamble, in return for habits, shoes and other essential commodities. The oyster beds of the river gave out in about 1870 and then fishermen turned to spratting. At one time there were 22 'spratters' operating out of the Hamble, but sprats went out of fashion and bumper catches could only be used for fertiliser in the strawberry fields for which this part of Hampshire is renowned.

There are still a few fishing boats which work from the Hamble, but today the river is dominated by yachting. At Warsash are premises of the **Royal Thames Yacht Club**, the oldest club in England. The clubhouse is also used by the Household Division Yacht Club, whose members are employed at Buckingham Palace. Each club on the river (and indeed, in the country) has its own distinctive pennant or burgee: The Hamble River SC has a red 'H' on blue and white. The Royal Southern YC has a crown on a red cross and the Royal Thames YC a crown on a white cross. The Household Division YC has a star on a red stripe. 'Burgee spotting' is a much neglected pastime!

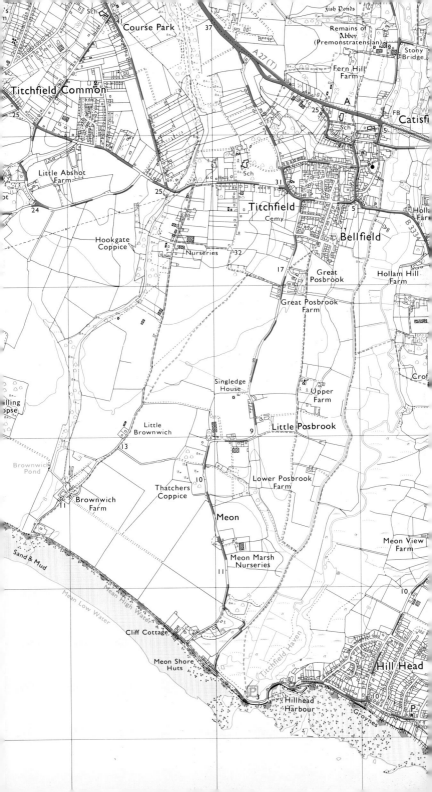

Fish Ponds

Remains of
Abbey
(Premonstratensian)

Course Park

37

A 27 (T)

Stony
Bridge

Fern Hill
Farm

Titchfield Common

A

25

25

Sch

5

Catisfi

Little Abshot
Farm

25

31

FB

Sch

Holl

24

ot

Titchfield

5

B 333

Cemy

Hookgate
Coppice

Nurseries

32

Bellfield

17

Great
Posbrook

Hollam Hill
Farm

Great Posbrook
Farm

Singledge
House

Upper
Farm

Crof

Little
Brownwich

13

9

Little Posbrook

Brownwich
Pond

illing
opse

Thatchers
Coppice

10

Lower Posbrook
Farm

11

Brownwich
Farm

Meon

Meon View
Farm

Sand & Mud

Meon Marsh
Nurseries

11

10

Mean Low Water

Mean High Water

Cliff Cottage

Titchfield Haven

Meon Shore
Huts

Hill Head

P

P
3

Hillhead
Harbour

10

Groynes

P

Above: Piper and Commandos at Warsash before embarkation.

Below: Beaches at Ouistreham near Caen where the Commandos under Lord Lovat landed June 6 1944.

A reminder of the part played in the last war by local boatyards is given by a plaque on the wall of the Rising Sun pub on the hard at Warsash. It records the D-Day embarkation of the landing craft of HMS *Tormentor*, a wartime establishment based at Stone Pier Yard close by the ferry terminus. Accompanied by the skirl of Brigadier Lord Lovat's personal piper, 3,000 commandos left the Hamble for the beaches of Normandy.

To ensure that the D-Day landings took place at the correct spot on the French coast, the beaches were marked by the crews of two midget submarines which left HMS *Dolphin*, Gosport, in advance of the main invasion. Two years earlier on March 15th the very first midget to be launched had slipped into the Hamble river under cover of darkness two miles above Warsash. Designed by Cdr Cromwell Varley, a retired naval officer, the prototype of these tiny craft was proven in trials in the Solent, returning each time to the security of a specially constructed catamaran on the Hamble.

The Solent Way continues along the shore towards the **College of Maritime Studies**, formerly called the Warsash School of Navigation, set up in 1935 by Captain G.W. Wakeford, a former master of the *Queen Mary*. Since these early days it has come to be one of the prime schools internationally for training Merchant Navy officers and has some of the most advanced equipment, including a bridge simulator.

Beyond the college the trail moves onto open coastlands which continue with scarcely a building for six miles. At Hook Lake one enters the Hook-with-Warsash Nature Reserve and there is another sanctuary for wildlife at Titchfield Haven. It is a shore where the walker can be on his own, if he wishes, for a couple of hours, but it might have been otherwise. At Warsash a hundred years ago there were three separate works on the shore — a 'chemical works' and sites for iron-smelting and cement manufacture. Further east on the Hook foreshore plans were put forward in 1943 by the Southampton Harbour Board for a combined sea and land airport. And in the late 1950s there were discussions about siting an oil refinery at Hook, which received a polite but determined 'raspberry' from the entire yachting world.

The only development which has been undertaken along this part of the Solent is a small group of holiday chalets at Solent Breezes. If proof be needed that the seas of the Solent area are constantly eating into the land, it can be seen here, where desperate measures are required to prevent the most seaward of the chalets being undermined by winter storms.

Further east the Solent Way moves to the cliffs of the **Brownwich** shore with farmland behind. Below Brownwich Farm, where a 'bunny' makes it easy to land a boat from the sea, can be seen well-preserved defences that are typical of the precautions taken all along the South Coast at any point where an enemy might have landed during the last war.

The Solent Way leads to **Titchfield Haven**, so called because it was once possible to navigate all the way up to Titchfield, home of the earls of Southampton. In the early years of the 17th century the Meon was closed at its mouth by the 3rd Earl who wanted to reclaim the estuary

david thelwell.

Birds of Titchfield Haven

and maintain a seaway to the village by means of a canal on the west bank, most of which survives. A lock was built at the seaward end of the New River, as the cut was called, and the main river was dammed with a huge shingle bank pierced by a sluice at Hill Head. But the bank did not endure and had to be replaced by a new barrier built closer to the sea. Eventually, in the 1890s, the canal was abandoned and diverted to the main river, which still has its flow regulated by a sluice. Remnants of the grand scheme can be seen to the north of the chalets of the Meon Shore, which are reached as the trail descends from Brownwich cliffs: stagnant water and a mass of reeds are all that remain of what was once called Posbrook Haven.

If the earl's intention had been to keep Titchfield open to sea traffic he failed. But it is likely that the New River was also built to create water meadows along the lower reaches of the Meon — and it has even been suggested that the earl may have wanted to make an ideal habitat for the wildfowl which he and his friends loved to shoot. If that was the case, he succeeded and must be credited with the extensive reed beds, saltings and marshes which now make up the Titchfield Haven Nature Reserve, where bird watchers can study one of the Solent's richest sites for migratory wildfowl. Since the Hampshire County Council took over the land in 1972, two lagoons have been dug and walkways and hides provided to penetrate the heart of the reserve.

Left to right: Ringed Plovers, Wigeon, Lapwing, Teal

The Solent Way continues along the coast to Hill Head and beyond, but if you wish there is an attractive six-mile detour to **Titchfield** and its abbey, along the banks of the canal. A footpath emerges in the village alongside the parish church, which is of great interest. Here can be seen a late 7th century Anglo-Saxon porch dating from the time when the Jutes, who settled in the Meon valley after the West Saxon invasions, had only just been converted to Christianity. The church also has a superb Norman doorway and a wealth of memorials, including the Wriothesley Monument, an impressive marble and alabaster tomb with three effigies by Gerard Johnson, a notable sculptor from Flanders who worked in England during Elizabethan times. The monument was erected in 1594 under the terms of the will of the 2nd Earl of Southampton to commemorate himself, his wife and his parents.

To the north of the village across the A27 Portsmouth-Southampton road is **Titchfield Abbey and Place House**. The abbey was founded in 1232 by Peter des Roches, the bishop of Winchester who also instigated Netley Abbey. At the dissolution the abbey and its lands were bought by Thomas Wriothesley, the 'asset stripper' who also acquired monastic properties at Beaulieu and elsewhere. Within days of the surrender of Titchfield by the order whose monks had held it for 300 years, Wriothesley was selling off altars, statues and other monastic valuables to local people. And within a few years he had had Place House (then called Palace house) built, much of which remains. Particularly striking is the Tudor gatehouse which was grafted onto the nave of the abbey church.

At Place House we come across another piece of the story of the flight of Charles I, for it was here that he stayed after an exhausting journey from London and hoped that he might seek sanctuary at Carisbrooke Castle on the Isle of Wight (see p. 10). As subsequent events showed, this was tantamount to walking into the lion's mouth and led to his imprisonment on the island and a forlorn return to London via Hurst.

Place House also has a connection with Shakespeare, for the 3rd Earl of Southampton — the one who closed Titchfield Haven — was his patron. But credible links with the area are hard to find. There are stories that some of the poet's plays were once performed in the grounds of Place House and that the plot of *Romeo and Juliet* was based on a local family feud. Even the name Gobbo, used in *The Merchant of Venice*, was at one time thought to be that of a Titchfield family recorded in the church registers; but it turns out to have been a misreading of 'Holte'. So tangible links between Titchfield and Shakespeare are probably no more than nice thoughts.

A mile above the abbey is the site of Funtley iron-mill where in 1603 the 3rd Earl set up an iron-making works closely connected with Sowley (see p. 25). Pig iron from the New Forest smeltworks was shipped to Funtley for forging into wrought iron. Later, what is reputed to be the first tin-plate mill in England was set up at Funtley for making girdles — a form of griddle — for the London market. But Funtley's name is probably best known for being the place where Henry Cort first showed how to purify iron and make it more workable by 'puddling' it with pit coal in a furnace. His work at Funtley in the early 1780s gave another little push to the Industrial Revolution, but the conditions for making best use of his inventions lay elsewhere, on the coalfields.

Titchfield today is best known for being the place where the National Census is compiled and analysed. And locally its carnival on Guy Fawkes Day is renowned: 'bonfire boys' lead a procession with lighted torches to the traditional burning close by the abbey grounds. It's as close to a riot as the law will allow!

HILL HEAD
TO
GOSPORT

Stokes Bay from Fort Gilkicker

HILL HEAD TO GOSPORT

The want of fine buildings, and grand colonnades,
Is made up by fine women, dear good-humoured jades;
Though the lasses of pleasure, take black, fair and brown,
Scarce amount to ten thousand in all Gosport town.

Henry Mann, 1802

Crossing the Meon river takes the trail to **Hill Head** alongside a tiny harbour which is one of the most attractive points on this part of the Solent coast. The basin scoured out by the river can be walked round in five minutes and has moorings for only a few boats, but it has the saltiness of Keyhaven or Eling and is an ideal place to while away time.

Hill Head looks across to the sloping lawns of Osborne House on the Isle of Wight, former home of Queen Victoria and Prince Albert. Here the full width of the waters of the East Solent is apparent and it is possible to appreciate the importance of such places as Lepe, where the island is a mere two miles from the mainland.

Ahead is a long shingle beach which stretches to the ramparts of Gosport and at **Lee-on-Solent** is backed by a concrete promenade for more than a mile. Here it is sometimes possible to imagine that one is on the Riviera, and the blocks of low-rise flats which have in recent years sprung up behind the prom add to the illusion.

The Solent Way approaches Lee past Scots Pine shaped by the wind and a deep shady cut through the cliff where the road from Stubbington descends to the beach. These trees are the last that will be seen beside the coast until the trail approaches its end. Indeed, the barrenness of this part of the Solent shore, in contrast to the leafy cover of the Netley foreshore and the New Forest, is one of its main characteristics and has given its name to the heath called Browndown, formerly Bare Down, which lies beyond Lee. But mere emptiness did not deter developers from exercising their imaginations. Nearly a century ago, a wealthy man from Swanage, Sir J.C. Robinson, spotted the Lee shore whilst cruising offshore with his son and decided that it should be developed into a resort. The key, so he thought, to making a success of the venture was to build a pier and connect it to the populous areas of Gosport and Portsmouth by a railway line. But Lee as a major resort never came about and the line was closed in 1935; only an amusements arcade and a line of beach huts remain to mark the former station and platform. At about this time the pierhead was developed by building an entertainments centre and a white tower 120-feet high, which for many years was a prominent landmark — some would say folly — around the Solent, until its demolition in 1969.

Although Lee has not prospered as a resort, it has become a popular residential area, particularly with Naval personnel from HMS

Daedalus and other establishments nearby. It is a reminder that from here on, until the Solent Way crosses the top of Langstone Harbour, we are in a part of Hampshire where the fortunes of the Services have dictated the local economy.

HMS *Daedalus* is the Fleet Air Arm's Training Establishment and is situated on an extensive airfield which dates back to 1910 when the Royal Flying Corps set up a small seaplane base at Lee. The hangars and slipways are still there and until recently were used by the Interservices Hovercraft Trials Unit, which proved the prototype SR.N1 hovercraft and other machines.

The prom at Lee comes to an abrupt end close to the Elmore Angling Club, (which has appeared in the *Guinness Book of Records* for mounting, jointly with the RNLI, the biggest beach-fishing competition in the country). It is a place to pause and look at the Island view, from the 180-foot spire of All Saints Church, Ryde (a resort that did prosper!) to Cowes Roads and the entrance to Southampton Water, where tankers often line up before making for the Esso oil refinery. Further west, there is a direct view down the entire length of the West Solent to Hurst almost twenty miles away.

Ahead is the **Browndown** firing range, a scene of military desolation with rusty narrow-gauge railways leading to huge shingle butts. It is an eerie landscape which has been used for military training for more than 300 years. Perhaps it is appropriate that it is the site of the last recorded duel between Englishmen, when Lt Hawkey of the Royal Marines fired at and mortally wounded Capt Seton of the 11th Dragoons to settle a matter of honour.

As the trail approaches **Stokes Bay**, No Man's Land Fort can be seen out to sea. And at the western end of the bay are the remains of a land fort and defensive lines running inshore towards Anglesey. These and the other works which will be seen as the Solent Way nears Portsmouth are signs of the massive efforts that have been made over the years to defend the Naval port from enemy attack. Perhaps the best way to understand the strategies of the military engineers who designed these defences is to visit Fort Brockhurst two miles to the north, where a museum sets out the details, but briefly it was like this.

As the range of gunnery increased it became necessary to extend the defences of Portsmouth progressively until the town and its hinterland was surrounded by a ring of forts that not only protected it from assaults from the sea but also from landward attacks from the west and encircling actions from the heights of the down at the head of the harbour. Following a royal commission of 1859, Palmerston decided against considerable opposition to put into action a plan for making Portsmouth impregnable. It involved 20 land forts and four forts built at sea and has been controversial ever since, some dubbing the defences 'Palmerston's follies'. At the far end of Stokes Bay is one of the forts strengthened at the time, Fort Gilkicker, which was armed with 20 guns with calibres up to 12" and seven 13" mortars.

The route of the path around the bay to this formidable position passes the remains of a pier which once provided a rail steamer service to Ryde. To the north can be seen The Crescent, a curving white terrace

Interior of HMS Alliance

of elegant houses built when the seaside resort of Anglesey was developed in the 1820s. In addition to a reading room and a bath-house, visitors were provided with the essentials of a watering place of the day, including bathing machines, a race course and regattas. Today Stokes Bay is still a place where local people go to enjoy themselves.

Fort Gilkicker is rather tumbledown, but it is still used — as a Royal Naval Observation Post. A climb to the top of the earthen ramparts which enclose it gives a superb view of the locality. Immediately to the north is a defensive moat, the remains of bogland which appears on old maps as Stokes Morass. To the east are the star-shaped bastions of Fort Monckton, which dates from the late 18th century, and is still in use. Beyond are the buildings of the Haslar Royal Naval Hospital with its distinctive water tower and HMS *Dolphin* at Fort Blockhouse, one of the oldest defences of Portsmouth Harbour, originally built in wood. To the north is Portsdown Hill. In the waters of Spithead there is a constant traffic of ships, ferries to the Isle of Wight or the Continent, Naval vessels and the occasional hovercraft running between Southsea and Ryde. When 'something big' is happening out in the roads, such as a Review of the Fleet or the Parade of Sail that accompanied the Cutty Sark Tall Ships' Races in 1982, this is the spot where people gather.

The Solent Way continues alongside Stoke Morass and then passes the entrance to Fort Monckton, where a telescopic triangular stone column stands: it is not a monument, nor a seamark but a giant apprentices' piece constructed in 1925 by Royal Engineers mason boys.

The path returns to the water at the edge of **Haslar Royal Naval Hospital**, where an impressive sloping sea wall runs all the way to Fort Blockhouse. This is an ideal vantage point from which to view the superb cityscape of Portsmouth, particularly the older part of the city.

'Holland I' and 'HMS Alliance'

At the mouth of the harbour on the other side is the delicate small green spire of Tower House, once the home and studio of the well-known marine painter, W.L. Wyllie. Alongside is the Round Tower and further east the Square Tower and the Saluting Platform, with the promenade stretching to Southsea Castle beyond. This is just a foretaste of the old fortified town of Portsmouth which grew up around the Camber dock and the Point.

Four distinctive landmarks poke up above the mass of the city — from left to right, the guildhall, the cathedral, the spire of St Jude's church, Southsea, and the Royal Naval War Memorial. Ahead on this shore is HMS *Dolphin*, an establishment which for nearly 80 years has been the headquarters of the Flag Officer Submarines in peacetime. In the square tower that dominates the site, 140′ high, submariners routinely learn how to escape underwater and return safely to the surface 100′ above.

The detailed story of *Dolphin* and submarines in general is told in the **Royal Navy Submarine Museum** nearby. On the way the path passes the former main entrance to the Haslar Royal Naval Hospital, built in the reign of George II (note the impressive royal coat of arms covering the central pediment) and the home of the Institute of Naval Medicine. Such men as Dr James Lind, a famous surgeon who promoted the treatment of scurvy, were working at Haslar more than a hundred years before the first stone was laid at the Army's equivalent institution at Netley.

The Submarine Museum's prize exhibits are the Navy's first submarine, 'Holland 1', and HMS *Alliance* a patrol class vessel which stands on concrete piles clear of the water. A tour of *Alliance* is preceded by a film briefing and parties are taken round the remarkably cramped space of the boat by former submariners. 'Holland 1', recovered from the sea-bed off the Eddystone Rock in 1982, is in the

81

Gosport from Portsmouth Hard

process of restoration and is the only surviving example of an invention of an Irish American, John Holland, whose original intention had been to devise a means of scuppering the British fleet in the Irish Cause! Said to be 'one yard shorter than a cricket pitch', HM Submarine No. 1 had the tear-drop shape to which the designers of nuclear submarines have returned in recent years.

Inside the Submarine Museum are many fascinating displays, including such items as the tiny safety pin taken from the torpedo that HMS *Conqueror* fired in the controversial sinking of the *General Belgrano* in the Falklands War of 1982.

The Solent Way continues across Haslar Lake towards **Gosport Hard**, past ramparts that date from the 17th century. The distinctive campanile (free-standing bell tower) of Holy Trinity Church is ahead and on the shore are two high-rise tower blocks with one of the finest views in the country. The abstract mosaic murals which stretch up the entire face of each block were a master stroke of Gosport architect, Edward Tyrell.

Gosport is the home of a number of Naval Establishments which 'spilled over' from the far side of the harbour. To the north of the Hard is the Royal Clarence Victualling Yard, and Priddy's Hard, the Royal Naval Armaments Depot, where gunpowder was first stored in 1771.

The trail now takes its fourth ferry, which leaves from a posh landing stage opened in 1983, the centenary year of the Portsmouth Harbour

Ferry Company. Waiting in comfort for the *Gosport Queen* or *Solent Enterprise* to dock gives the walker a few moments to examine the vista of Portsmouth Dockyard and its surroundings. But first note the yard of Camper and Nicholsons on the Gosport side, boatbuilders extraordinaire and world famous for a stream of famous craft, including Sir Francis Chichester's *Gipsy Moth IV*.

The ferry makes for a stage alongside the Isle of Wight steamers. To the north is the dockyard, fronted by the Semaphore Tower with its prominent flagstaff, where the Flag Officer Portsmouth has his offices. The docks, slipways, stores and workshops of the dockyard stretch up into the harbour. In the distance, three miles above the dockyard, may be seen Portchester Castle, where the Romans docked their ships.

To the south of the dockyard is HMS *Vernon*, famous for torpedo warfare but due to be closed in 1986 as part of Naval rationalisation plans. Another familiar establishment, HMS *Excellent,* which stands on the land reclaimed at Whale Island a hundred years ago, is also due to shut down. Major changes such as these have often been faced by the people of Gosport and Portsmouth, but the area has probably never been better placed to cope, for light industry and leisure services have come and taken root in recent years.

PORTSM

PORTSMOUTH

PORTSMOUTH

*The town of Portsmouth is measured from the
east tower a furrow length, with a mud wall armed with
timber, whereon lie pieces of iron and brass*

John Leland, 1540

Like brothers entering Church and Army, the Solent's two cities
have gone different ways: for Southampton Docks read HM
Naval Base Portsmouth.

The future of the Naval port was settled by the Tudor kings, Henry
VII and Henry VIII, who built a dry dock on the present site of the dockyard and set up workshops for shipwrights and other craftsmen. Before
the establishment of a permanent navy, there were few fighting ships;
some were built at Southampton and moored in the Hamble river,
where the wreck of one of them, the *Grâce Dieu* still lies.

Most of the dockyard which can be seen at Portsmouth today dates
from the 18th century and later. One of the oldest features is the Main
Gate, topped with two huge gilded balls, which remained a narrow
entrance until the end of the war, when it was widened 'to meet the
needs of modern road traffic'. Access inside the base is limited, but
civilians can visit the Royal Naval Museum, housed in former
storehouses, and the prime exhibits of this historic site, HMS *Victory*
and the *Mary Rose*. The old boat-houses and, to the north, the former
ropehouse — which is more than a thousand feet in length — are just a
few of the remaining works that were built at Portsmouth during the
18th century, when the growing menace of France and Spain
heightened the strategic importance of Spithead and the dockyard.

The story of the excavation of the *Mary Rose* on the bed of Spithead
by marine archaeologist Margaret Rule and a team of divers has attracted national attention in recent years. The remains of the timber hull
are now preserved in an humidified enclosure alongside the *Victory*
and many of the artefacts recovered are on exhibition in No. 5
Boathouse, just inside the main gate of the dockyard.

The *Mary Rose*, built 250 years before *Victory* in the year that Henry
VIII came to the throne, was the victim of an attempted invasion by the
French in 1545 to revenge the recent capture of Boulogne by the British.
An armada of ships under Admiral D'Annibault sailed up the Channel
and anchored off St Helen's on the Isle of Wight. Their hope was to land
60,000 French troops on the island and from there launch an attack on
the mainland. Henry VIII was with the British commander, Lord Lisle,
on board the *Henry Grâce à Dieu* at Portsmouth when the threat
became known. He hastily disembarked to watch the action from the
safety of Southsea Castle.

The battle itself is of interest for being one of the last between old-
fashioned but manoeuvreable French galleys propelled by oar and the

The 'Mary Rose'

galleons, which the British favoured. In the event the French attack was fought off, but during the mêlée the *Mary Rose* suddenly heeled over and sank, with the loss of her entire crew of 700 and her commander, Sir John Carew. To this day, no one knows why the accident happened, though it may have been due to a failure to close the lower gun ports when tacking.

An immediate attempt to salvage the ship failed and it was not until 1836 that any sign of her was seen again. In that year two remarkable brothers, John and Charles Deane, who had adapted their father's fire-fighting suit for deep-sea diving, found the wreck of the *Mary Rose* after fishermen complained of snagging their nets on timbers. Although they found enough relics to identify the ship positively, and John Deane recorded them in his own superb water-colours, the position of the site had been lost once more when Alexander McKee, a journalist and amateur diver, decided in 1965 to try to find some of the old wrecks lost in the Solent. Only the chance finding of an old chart in the Hydrographer's Department of the Royal Navy with the Deanes' discovery marked on it enabled the wreck to be found once more.

The finds from the *Mary Rose*, many of which are on display in No. 5 Boathouse, provide a unique view of Tudor life. There are examples of cannister shot (wooden containers filled with flints) and longbows; a leather bucket with that familiar mark of War Department property, an arrow, scribed on the side — and the tools of a barber surgeon: a syringe for treating venereal disease, drug flasks and much else. Also on show are crudely-made gaming boards, a wooden tankard or tigg, a pocket sundial and navigational instruments. Moreover, a reconstruction of two of the ship's gun-decks and a replica of the barber-surgeon's cabin portray some aspects of life aboard the Tudor warship.

VEHICLE (V) & FOOT PASSENGER (F) FERRIES

SHIP

Le Havre (V/F)	5½ hrs
Cherbourg (V/F) (Summer only)	4½-6½ hrs
St Malo (V/F)	8½-10 hrs
Guernsey (V/F)	6½-7 hrs
Jersey (V/F)	9-9½ hrs

Fountain Lake

Mean High Water

HMS Excellent

Pier

Piers

Boro Const Bdy

Groyne

ardway

Mast

Mean High Water

Sch

North Corner

HM Dockyard

Burrow Island

Pier Weevil Lake

Jetty

HMS Victory

Portsea

SPORT

Dismtd Rly

Sch

Newtown

Mus

FB

Yacht Marina

Sta

Ferry F

Recn Gd

HMS Vernon

Coll

Cockle Pond

Haslar Lake

Seafield

HMS Hornet

Haslar Bridge

HMS Dolphin

The Point

Square Tower

Old Portsmouth

Coll

Sch

Mus

Gosport Park

Stoke Lake

Clayhall

Cemy

Fort Blockhouse

Groynes

Royal Naval Hospital Haslar

Euro Const & Boro Const Bdy

FB

Clarence Pier

Hovercraft Terminal

PC Meml

So Co

A 288

FOOT PASSENGER FERRY HOVERCRAFT

Ryde   7 mins

HM Detention Centre

Club

Mean Low Water

Spit Sand

Fort Monckton

FOOT PASSENGER FERRY

SHIP

Ryde   25-30 mins

VEHICLE (V) & FOOT PASSENGER (F) FERRY

SHIP

Fishbourne (V/F)   ¾ hr

Groynes

(PORTSMOUTH DISTRI
PORTSMOUTH SOUTH BORO

Nelson and 'HMS Victory'

The exhibition makes plain that the ship was built after naval architects had found a technical solution to the problem of mounting large numbers of heavy guns below decks. She was therefore an example of the 'new technology' of her day and to see her disappear beneath the waters of Spithead must have brought grave doubts to the Tudor king and his advisers. They need not have feared, for Tudor enterprise led ultimately to HMS *Victory*, preserved in No. 2 Dry Dock, a great ship which still requires many of the commodities worked by the traditional craftsmen of the dockyard: hemp, tar, caulking, ironwork, masts, blocks — and much else besides. There are regular conducted tours below the ship's decks, but note also the external details, particularly the intricate carving and joinery of the stern.

The *Victory* was, of course, the man-of-war which flew Nelson's flag at the Battle of Trafalgar. Indeed, it still is in commission as the flagship of the Commander-in-Chief Naval Home Command. As remarkable as its fighting record is the fluke by which *Victory* stayed afloat (just!) for more than a hundred years after she was paid off. She was moored around the harbour for a variety of purposes and it was only due to the efforts of the Society for Nautical Research and others that she was eventually saved and restored in 1928.

Before leaving the *Victory* look at the dry dock in which she rests, or even better the unoccupied dock to the west. The ability to work on ships from the stone steps of basins like these, sliding materials to the shipwrights below, was why naval commanders like Nelson brought back their ships to Portsmouth for repairs. By comparison, commercial masters had to make do with much more primitive facilities until the 19th century.

The full story of British naval warfare is admirably told in the **Royal Naval Museum** housed in the elegant 18th century storehouses that stand along the road from the Main Gate. There is a whole gallery devoted to Nelson and his career, with many exhibits, including letters to his mistress, Lady Emma Hamilton, and a superb bowl presented by

the Danes after the Battle of Copenhagen — during which the famous commander put a telescope to his blind eye to avoid unwelcome orders. Note also the superb panorama of Trafalgar by W.L. Wyllie.

Other galleries cover almost the entire history of the Navy, from wars with the French (note the rare 'cap of liberty' captured from a ship in 1796) up to the Falklands War. The coming of steam and the growth of the specialist branches, such as chaplains and hydrographers, are dealt with in great detail. And some of the zanier inventions are described, such as Gunner Robert Whitby's 'oil shells' for aiding rescue operations by calming the waves. There is Lord Mountbatten's 'No. 5 Uniform Coat', the Beira Bucket recalling Rhodesia's declaration of UDI and a wealth of exhibits of medals and memorabilia from many campaigns fought by the Navy.

On leaving the dockyard note the huge figurehead of HMS *Warrior*, carved at Cowes by craftsmen Jack Whitehead and Norman Gaches. This is in fact a copy made for the Ship Preservation Trust which is restoring the vessel in time for 1986, when she will be berthed outside the dockyard gates alongside the Common Hard.

Like the *Victory*, the *Warrior* has been saved in the nick of time. Launched in 1850, she was the Navy's first ironclad and England's answer to the *Gloire* built two years earlier by the French. She was powered by both sail and steam and proved herself capable of reaching more than 14 knots, an unbeatable speed for the time. When her active life was over she became *Vernon III* and was moored in Portsmouth Harbour as a floating torpedo school. Then came ignominy and a long tow to Pembroke Dock where she became *Hulk C77*, an ordinary oil pontoon. Despite being half-filled with concrete her wrought iron hull has survived and is being restored at Hartlepool.

Warrior will further enhance Portsmouth's growing reputation as a major centre of Naval history, and there are plans to bring in more ships, including the *Foudroyant*, a teak-hulled man-of-war built in the Naval dockyard Bombay a few years after Trafalgar and now used as a training ship in the harbour. She is the oldest ship afloat in the world.

From the dockyard the Solent Way proceeds to **The Point**, a legendary area of Old Portsmouth where sailors went to let their hair down in a way that only sailors know how — hence its popular name, Spice Island (or was it due to the smell?). On the way the path passes the edge of **The Camber**, a small natural dock used by fishing boats and trading vessels since the 12th century. At the south end of the dock is a small yard belonging to Vosper Thornycroft, famous for its work with fast patrol boats. Set up in 1870 by Herbert Vosper, the company became a fierce competitor of the British Power Boat Company, Hythe, during the 1930s. They built one of Malcolm Campbell's *Bluebird* boats, which broke the World Water Speed Record in 1939.

The Camber is looked over by the Queen Anne cupola of the **cathedral**, which until the year after Portsmouth gained city status in 1926 was the parish church. It is a small, intimate building — not least because plans to extend it were cut short by the war, hence the red-brick 'temporary' west wall of the nave — and it is full of relics which

Walls of Old Portsmouth, looking towards the Square Tower

reflect the heritage of the city. The oldest part of the building dates from the late 1180s when the Norman merchant who founded the Camber dock, John de Gisors, gave land to Augustinian priors from Southwick — the small village behind Portsdown Hill from which Eisenhower masterminded D-Day operations (see p. 100).

The church was dedicated to Thomas à Becket, murdered in 1170, an event which recalls two notorious local killings which took place close by the church. The first, in 1450, so distressed the Pope that the town was excommunicated and mass could not be performed for more than fifty years — and then only when the vicar of St Thomas's and his congregation had been scourged barefoot from the church and readmitted on their knees. The crime for which this penance was exacted was the murder of Adam Moleyns bishop of Chichester, who had come on behalf of Henry VI to negotiate with seamen about unpaid wages. Their anger rose when they discovered that they would not be fully paid and they murdered the bishop, in what is now Grand Parade, at the foot of the High Street.

The second well-known murder at Portsmouth was carried out in the High Street itself, at No. 11, now called Buckingham House, where Charles II's favourite, the Duke of Buckingham, was stabbed to death by a lieutenant whose application for promotion he had rejected. There is a monument to Buckingham, a very unpopular man with the people, which carries the inscription (in Latin): *You, traveller, if you have any bowels of pity, groan with indignation.*

The cathedral's strong links with the Royal Navy are displayed in its Navy Aisle, which is beside the south wall to the right of the porch. Here is a list of the battles fought by all the ships called HMS *Mary Rose*, a fragment of the White Ensign flown by HMS *Victory* at Trafalgar and many other items. Close by is a copy of the elaborate entry made in the parish register at the time of the marriage of Charles II in the Governor's house nearby. And near the font on the north side of the tower is the cathedral's most valuable treasure, a plaque of the

Madonna and child by the famous Florentine sculptor, Andrea della Robbia, dating from about 1500. Look also, in the South Tower Transept, for the painting by W. L. Wyllie, whose former house with its prominent green spire is beside the Round Tower.

The trail goes to the tip of The Point, past The Lone Yachtsman, a pub named after Alec (later Sir Alec) Rose, the Portsmouth grocer who sailed single handed round the world. This is an ideal vantage point to look again at the harbour and the Gosport shore: Fort Blockhouse opposite, the square escape tower of HMS *Dolphin* and the Haslar Royal Naval Hospital with its prominent water tower. Up in the harbour is the Camper and Nicholson marina, the Royal Clarence Victualling Yard and the last vestiges of the woodland which was once to be seen on the shores of Portsmouth Harbour and is now confined to Borrow Island.

Close at hand is the former gunwharf where HMS *Vernon* has been based since 1923. This well-known establishment, which will close in 1986, started as an offshoot of the gunnery school, HMS *Excellent* when Jackie Fisher — later a famous Admiral of the Fleet — was given command of an old hulk fitted up as a training ship for torpedo warfare. *Vernon* has been in the thick of all aspects of this deadly activity, from the earliest use of explosive charges fixed at the end of booms to the self-propulsive Whitehead torpedo carried by 'coastal motor boats', then 'motor torpedo-boats' (MTBs) and, of course, submarines. Vosper's nearby often worked with the Navy on the design of MTBs, particularly during the 1930s, when the company was run by a retired naval officer, Commander Peter du Cane.

Although, as we have noted, Portsmouth and Southampton have developed separately, there is at least one major similarity — they both grew from fortified medieval towns beside the sea: **Old Portsmouth** is a counterpart of Southampton's Below Bar district. But in the naval port only the seaward margin of the defences is left. From The Point, eastwards to the stump of Clarence Pier are the well-preserved remains of works which once enclosed the old town, stretching north-east to the edge of what is now the United Services Recreation Ground, with the High Street as its main thoroughfare. Officers such as Nelson would stay in the George Hotel and then leave for their ships anchored offshore from the Sally Port at the entrance to Broad Street (though when he left for Trafalgar he attempted to dodge the crowds by leaving from Penny Street nearby!).

The defences which can be seen today — the Round Tower, the Eighteen Gun Battery, the Square Tower, the Saluting Platform, Long Curtain and King's Bastion — date from different periods. The oldest part is the Round Tower, built in 1418, and much of the rest is attributable to the Dutch engineer, Sir Bernard de Gomme, who in 1665 was commissioned to strengthen the defences of the town. Note also Capstan Square, alongside the Round Tower, where a great chain was stretched across to Fort Blockhouse to protect the harbour in Tudor times: a few of the huge links can be seen in the museum at Southsea Castle.

Close by the Square Tower is a monument in the form of a huge knot which commemorates the sailing from Spithead in 1787 of the first Australian settlers: what it omits to say on the accompanying plaque is that they were all convicts.

To the west of the Square Tower is Grand Parade and the shell of the Royal Garrison Church, formerly a wayfarer's hospice, *Domus Dei*, founded in 1212 by the instigator of the abbeys at Titchfield and Netley, Peter des Roches. After the dissolution *Domus Dei* became the home of the Governor of Portsmouth and here in 1662 Charles II married Catherine of Braganza of Portugal in return for a dowry of £300,000 and the naval bases of Tangier and Bombay. The marriage was entered in the parish register of St Thomas's church, now the cathedral, as mentioned above.

The Royal Garrison Church was destroyed by fire after an air raid in 1941 and it now stands as a permanent reminder of the days when German attacks gutted vast areas of Portsmouth and Gosport. With the invention of the aeroplane the elaborate defences of de Gomme and Palmerston became virtually valueless, and ever since the Ministry of Defence have exercised much ingenuity in trying to make use of the forts that pepper the Solent shores.

In the churchyard of the former *Domus Dei* is the grave of Sir Charles Napier, a distinguished soldier and colonial administrator who in 1843 captured Hyderabad and annexed what is now the Sind province of Pakistan. To announce his victory he sent a one-word dispatch which merely read '*peccavi*', which is Latin for 'I have sinned' — surely the most awful pun ever!

Also in the churchyard is an iron mortar which commemorates the gathering of the Allied Sovereigns at Portsmouth in 1814 at the end of the Napoleonic Wars. The long period of peace which this signified was not good news for many local people, for within a few years a shortage of repair work in the dockyard meant that mechanics and labourers with up to 50 years' service had to be paid off, and the pay of those remaining was reduced.

Beyond the church is Governor's Green and the Long Curtain, a fine example of the moated defences of the fortified town built by de Gomme in the 17th century. At the eastern end is the arrow-shaped King's Bastion, reconstructed in 1703 and named after George II. Until 1931 a gun was fired here each day at sunset, whilst a one-o-clock gun resounded from the Long Curtain until the last war.

The Solent Way continues to Clarence Pier, where an arcade offers candy floss, hot dogs, bingo and video games. It is a sign that we are about to enter the fun quarter of the city, Southsea — one of the 'four towns' which traditionally make up the city: the others are Old Portsmouth, Landport and Portsea.

SOUTHSEA, EASTNEY & HAYLING ISLAND

SOUTHSEA, EASTNEY & HAYLING ISLAND

*With historic Portsmouth and modern Southsea combined,
it is difficult to imagine a better holiday resort,
at least for those who love their
fellow-humans.*

R.L.P. and Dorothy M. Jowitt, 1978

Despite the enormous importance of the Royal Navy to Portsmouth, the activities of the Senior Service have largely been confined to the south-west corner of Portsea Island. Until the rapid growth of the town in the last century, the land beyond Clarence Pier was open commons, marsh and fields. It was, however, defended by Southsea Castle and three other more recent forts built on the Eastney shore.

The essential character of **Southsea** as a fashionable suburb and seaside resort started in the early 19th century, but the heart of the place — where well-to-do people had a villa for the summer and naval officers rented an elegant house — was created later. Between 1837 and 1860 a developer and architect of genius, Thomas Ellis Owen, built the terraces and villas which lie to the north of Southsea Common and Clarence Parade and are bounded by Western Parade and Victoria Road South. Here, looked over from 1851 by the soaring spire of St Judes church, built at his expense, Owen exercised a talent for making an atmosphere which delighted the Victorian upper middle classes. And on the shore were the facilities that they sought: bathing machines and the baths and reading room at King's Rooms, on the present site of **Clarence Pier**. There was even snipe shooting for the men at Eastney and the newly drained common, where the drilling of garrison troops gave reassurance and made military men feel at home.

Later, Southsea acquired several stately hotels and piers — Clarence Pier in 1861 and the much longer South Parade Pier nearly twenty years later. The latter was burned down in 1904 and rebuilt within a few years by the Corporation — a superb investment, for **South Parade Pier** acted as a vital focus between the wars, when Southsea became a place where more and more ordinary people came for holidays.

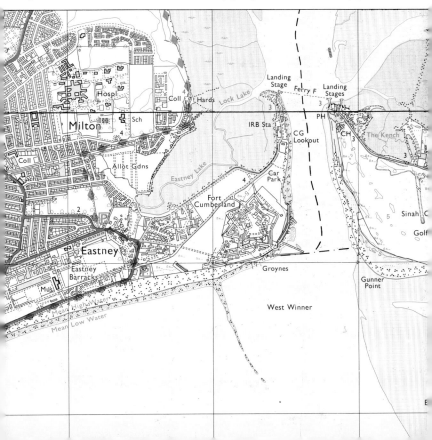

Troops awaiting D-Day: a display in the new museum.

The Solent Way leads to **Southsea Castle** whose ramparts hold the **D-Day Museum**, one of the area's most recent attractions. Opened forty years after the Normandy landings of June 1944 which spearheaded the Allied invasion of Europe, the museum tells the story of that period between Dunkirk and the end of the war, when Britain's future as a nation seemed to be at stake. The displays concentrate on the logistics, the politics — and the squabblings — of the operation, with particular emphasis on the contribution of the Solent locality.

There are some spectacular effects, including a simulation of what it was like to get ashore from a landing craft under fire. There is also a copy of the operations map used at Southwick House by General Eisenhower, comprehensive audio-visual presentations (in English, French and German) and a Vehicle Shed with examples of a DUKW, a Sherman Tank and one of the jeeps ferried across to the French coast by glider.

The centrepiece exhibit of the museum is the Overlord Embroidery, a pictorial record of the story of D-Day in 34 panels with a total extent of 272 feet, 40 feet longer than the Bayeux Tapestry. Designed by Sandra Lawrence and commissioned by Lord Dulverton, this magnificent memorial was made by twenty craft workers from the Royal School of Needlework, London, during the period 1968-73.

Nearby in Southsea Castle is another museum with displays on the maritime history and archaeology of the Portsmouth area, with several items of particular interest: a painting of Sir William Paulet (see p. 61), part of the great chain that protected Portsmouth harbour at one time and a Van Dyck portrait of Colonel George Goring, a Governor of Portsmouth whose dissolute ways helped to lose the town to the Parliamentarians during the Civil War. Note also the display on the defences of Portsmouth and in particular the building of Fort Cumberland and Hilsea Lines to prevent attacks from the east and north, respectively.

Southsea Castle

The archaeological section of the castle's museum shows a number of interesting finds from excavations carried out in Oyster Street, close to the Camber Dock. There are also maps of the Solent area recording where prehistoric remains have been found: these emphasise that Palaeolithic man lived close to the shore, where food could be found, whereas Neolithic man moved to the hinterland to cultivate the land and grow crops.

Incidently, although Southsea Castle dates from 1544, the arms over the main entrance are those of Charles II, put up at the time that Sir Bernard de Gomme strengthened the fort and the defences of Portsmouth in general.

The Solent Way continues along the sea front past the remains of Lumps Fort, now a rose garden. Out to sea can be seen some of the 'follies' built by Palmerston — Spit Sand Fort to the west, followed by No Man's Land Fort and Horse Sand Fort. They all stand in shallow water with their own artesian wells and were built in granite and Portland stone, protected by more than 15 inches of soft iron. To the southeast, eight miles away, can be seen a well-known navigational mark, Nab Tower — and at night the lights of a host of other aids, each with their definitive 'winking' pattern, can be picked out. Note that, for the first time since leaving Hurst, the horizon is not marked with the comforting contours of the Isle of Wight.

Ahead is the **Eastney Shore** and beyond Hayling Island, though the break of the Langstone Channel is hard to see. Inland is the distinctive clock tower of Eastney Barracks, which used to be a major Royal Marines base. The main gate is beneath the clock and this is the entrance to the barracks' key attraction, the **Royal Marines Museum**. This is housed in the former officers' mess, a mid-Victorian building of unusual grandeur with a feeling of Colonial largesse, which is said to have been finished so lavishly because a civil servent added a nought to the estimates! The museum's exhibits themselves are equally lavish

101

Display of Arctic warfare in the Royal Marines Museum

Eastney Pumping station

and tell the story of the Marines from 1664 to the present day.

A particularly topical exhibit is a number of relics from the 1982 South Atlantic Campaign, including an operations map from the final phase of the battle for Port Stanley used by Major General Jeremy (now Sir Jeremy) Moore.

Island wars feature prominently in the heritage of Marines: their Corps crest incorporates the word 'Gibraltar' in memory of their taking the famous rock in three days in July 1704, and a laurel wreath which is probably associated with the capture of Belle Isle, near Nantes, more than fifty years later. The museum has a large animated exhibit of the taking of Gibraltar and there are several other campaigns displayed with audiovisual effects, including the Battle of Jutland and the blocking of the canal at Zeebrugge. The Zeebrugge attack, which took place on St George's Day 1918, was particularly ingenious and is a classic combined Royal Navy-Royal Marines operation, several coordinated events bringing off the seemingly impossible. But the cost was enormous — 132 Marines killed. VCs won by the commander of the force which stormed the mole and by a sergeant, both awarded by a ballot of the battalion, can be seen in the museum's Medal Room.

There are many other exhibits in the museum covering a great range of topics, such as the development of commando tactics and snow warfare, a female marine who escaped detection for five years, marines at Trafalgar, uniforms, bands history and much else. One of the nastiest exhibits is a Japanese booby trap in the shape of a book entitled *Famous Nudes*.

The Solent Way continues past the approach to **Fort Cumberland**, the finest surviving example of an 18th-century defence work, with its bastions arranged in the shape of a five-pointed star. It was armed with eight 24-pounder guns and 73 other heavy weapons and built to defend the eastern approaches to Portsea Island. The fort is still occupied by the Services, though plans for opening it to the public have been discussed. The uniforms of the original garrison are often to be seen at Old Portsmouth, where a military revivalist group called the Fort Cumberland Guard performs parades.

At the top of Eastney Lake the trail passes a site of unusual importance for a subject that most of us like to forget — sewage (see p.116). **Eastney Pumping Station** has been operated since organised sewage disposal came to Portsmouth in 1868. The first set of pumps do not survive but two beam engines made by James Watt & Co. dating from 1886 can still be seen in their original house, a grand structure bearing the Corporation crest and looking like a Dissenter's chapel. The technicalities do not have to be understood to appreciate the monumental scale of the engineering. At weekends during the summer one of the engines is 'steamed' and then the huge flywheels, 15 feet in diameter, and the pistons of the old pumps can be seen in action. Each engine disposed of 250,000 gallons of sewage per hour, which was stored in tanks and let out at the entrance to Langstone Harbour on the outgoing tide.

Beyond the pumping station the trail continues up into the harbour, an abrupt change which trades the forts and seaside excitement of Southsea for the 'back' of Portsea Island. This was the route taken by officer Marines from Eastney Barracks who on a Sunday would walk to the bridge at Langstone and then across **Hayling Island** to the south-west corner, where they would row back to Portsmouth. Although the Solent Way does not cross to the island, taking the motor ferry and walking to the road bridge is an alternative way of reaching the top of the harbour. The fierce currents which race through the narrow entrance somehow manage to keep the shingle at Eastney and the sand on Hayling! Indeed, one of the island's greatest assets is its sandy beaches, which according to *White's Directory* of 1859, are 'so firm that carriage wheels make but a faint impression'.

The sandy beaches of South Hayling were much used during the last war by Combined Operations Pilotage Parties to practise landing operations in preparation for D-Day.

Hayling Island today is probably best known for being a windsurfing centre. Moreover, the sport was invented here in 1958 by 12-year-old Peter Chilvers, whilst 'messing about' on holiday at Mengham on the east of the island. When he grew up he made a business out of his invention, which has of course spread round the world. Northney is now the focus of windsurfing on Hayling and has played host to world championships. It was also at Northney that the first of another Hayling institution, the holiday camp, was opened in the mid-1920s by Warner's, who came to own four other camps on the island, including an early Civil Service camp which could not be made to pay by its first owners.

One of the drawbacks of Hayling for the visitor in the 1920s was the vast number of mosquitoes which bred in the saltings and marshes on the island and swarmed on the beaches. To tackle the problem, a resident and an expert on British mosquitoes, John Marshall, set up Hayling Mosquito Control, an organisation for collecting and destroying the eggs of the insects.

An important event in opening Hayling to visitors was the building of a toll bridge in 1824, a predecessor of the present link with the mainland and on the site of a wadeway which in ancient times was tended by a hermit. (Caution: the channel has since been deepened!) One of the promoters was William Padwick who shortly acquired the manor of Hayling (most of the island) and laid plans to turn it into a fashionable and profitable resort. If Southsea nearby had not been blossoming at the same time he might have succeeded, but as it was Hayling was never more than a minor attraction until holidays became universal.

The remains of the old railway bridge alongside Langstone Bridge are a reminder of the 'Crab and Winkle' line which ran from Havant to the south of the island between 1867 and 1963. The old track now serves as a footpath up the western shore. But the route which takes the walker through the heart of Hayling would probably take in the south of the island and the sea-front, including the uncompleted Crescent dating from about 1830, and then turn to Northney and North Hayling, via Beach Road and the Manor House, from which William Padwick ruled his estate — mainly by writ!

Section XI

LANGSTONE HARBOUR & EMSWORTH

Langstone Harbour

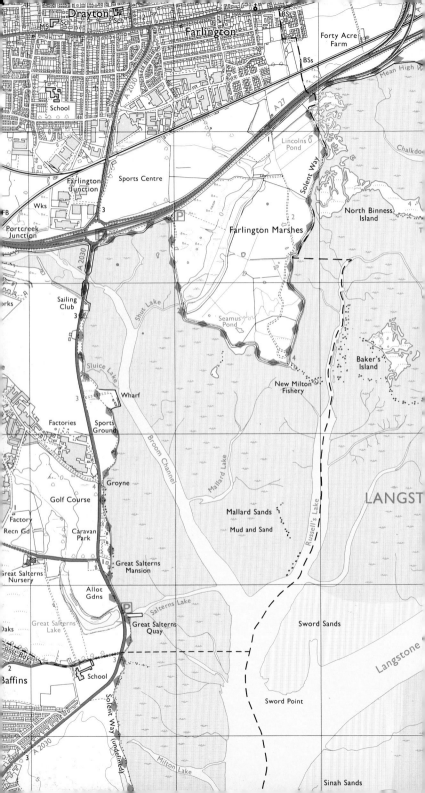

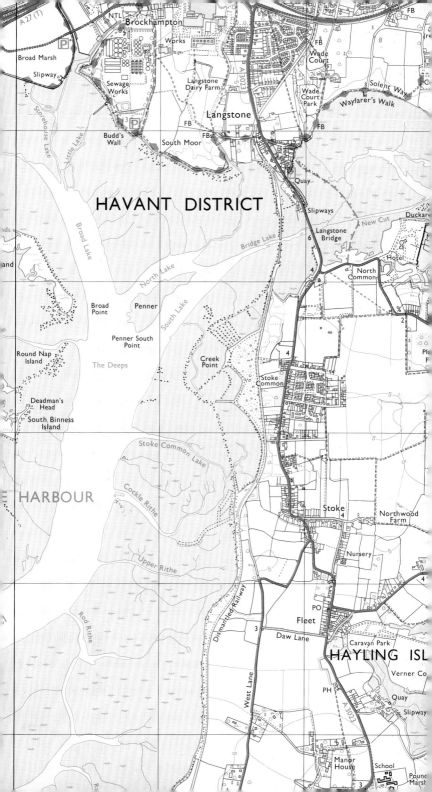

LANGSTONE HARBOUR & EMSWORTH

He was a bold man who first ever swallowed an oyster

James I quoted by Jonathan Swift

Nearly five thousand acres of tidal water and mudbanks, a shoreline of 16 miles, many thousands of wildfowl and a natural wealth of marine life — all these make **Langstone Harbour** an area of outstanding interest and importance. It is one of the few Solent lakes which has kept its emptiness, and life on its waters is much the same as it has always been. It has been a harbour for the little boats, carrying a cargo of shellfish or Hayling Bay mackerel, or a load of bricks or ballast.

As the name suggests, the traditional port of call for most of the vessels entering the narrow straits between Eastney and Hayling was Langstone, which stands at the head of the harbour. But this attractive spot, once the port of Havant, no longer has any trade and what activity there is in the harbour is at the few Portsea wharves and further east at Emsworth. Any plans for developing the harbour beyond a local facility have always had to contend with the shallowness of its waters and the bar which exists outside its mouth. One scheme proposed in 1908 by the Portsmouth Chamber of Commerce involved dredging the bar and using the spoil to build a quay along the eastern edge of Portsea Island, with wet and dry docks and a timber basin — but nothing came of it.

An earlier venture to use the harbour as part of an inland route to London was put into operation but was not successful. At the Portsmouth end there was a canal, the route of which is followed by the Solent Way where it turns off Ironbridge Road (note the name) in the Milton district of Portsmouth close to Eastney Lake. The canal entered the sea alongside the modern premises of the Langstone Harbour Fishermen's Association, where some stonework and traces of the lock gates can be seen. Completed in 1823, the canal ran to a basin in the centre of Portsmouth and was intended to provide a link with the capital via the rivers Arun, Wey and Thames. But the complicated series of locks, transshipments and tolls was cumbersome and the canal was finally made obsolete by the coming of the railways.

Alongside the aptly named Locks Sailing Club there is good view of the harbour and its surroundings. Opposite on Sinah Sands is a huge broken-backed caisson which failed to make it to the Normandy coast for use in building one of the Mulberry harbours. The Eastney-Hayling Island ferry is immediately ahead, with the island stretching away and the South Downs beyond. At the top of the harbour is a prominent chimney: it belongs to a monster refuse incinerator at Brockhampton.

Solent Way at Milton

Nearby in Eastney Lake are the boats of the many fishermen who work (and play!) in these waters.

At low water the branching pattern of the 'lakes' of Langstone Harbour emerge. But note that in the northern reaches of the harbour the dialect word 'rithe' is used, as the map shows.

A large part of the eastern side of Portsea Island has been reclaimed from the sea. The rather empty piece of land to the north of Milton Lock was made up in recent years by filling Velder Lake, a creek which wound up to the former village of Milton. Another scheme in the vicinity of **Great Salterns Quay** was carried out as long ago as 1680 and for this reason is marked on old maps as being 'extra-parochial'. In this part of Portsmouth and on Hayling Island a substantial area of salt works existed, but neither site was as extensive as that at Lymington (see p. 17). Portsea salterns provided an essential commodity for the dockyard, and were Crown property until 1830.

Above the old salterns at the southern edge of the former city airport, closed in 1973, is the factory which Nevile Norway (better known as Nevile Shute) built for Airspeed Aviation in the early 1930s. This company brought aircraft manufacture to Portsmouth, producing such models as the Airspeed Envoy and Airspeed Oxford, and also the Horsa gliders used for the invasion of Normandy and the Battle of Arnhem. In the late 1930s Portsmouth Corporation, who had totally failed to make any headway with plans for docks in Langstone Har-

Farlington Marshes

bour, tried to interest Imperial Airways and the Air Ministry in operating commercial flying boats from the area. But fears of war scotched the idea, which later experience (see p.45) showed would in any event have been a flop.

At the top of the harbour the Solent Way follows round the perimeter of **Farlington Marshes**, a nature reserve run by the Hampshire and Isle of Wight Naturalists Trust and renowned for the richness of its birdlife. Off the eastern shore of the marsh is a group of salt-marsh islands (where, incidently, rich prehistoric finds have been discovered) which form another reserve operated by the RSPB. Here on South Binness and Round Nap Islands there are important breeding colonies of ringed plover and little tern, together with more common species such as mallard, oystercatcher and redshank. On the marshes and at a large number of spots around the harbour can be seen a wide range of species of wildfowl and waders, particularly during the winter months when large numbers of birds from colder latitudes come to Langstone. Ironically, it is believed that the discharge of sewage into the harbour has helped to produce the rich growths of algae and eelgrass on which some of the birds feed, notably dark-bellied brent geese and wigeon. It has been estimated that three per cent or more of the world's population of this species of goose come each year from the Russian sub-arctic to winter in Langstone Harbour.

Langstone

More birds will be seen further along the trail at **Brockhampton** where a tip seething with gulls is part of a group of essential services situated around a working quay. In a short distance the path returns once more to tranquility and runs into **Langstone**. This is now under the jurisdiction of the Chichester Harbour Conservancy but was at one time the eastern limit of the Port of Southampton (yes, Southampton!), which spread westwards as far as Lymington. But Langstone's trading days are over, though much of the quay survives alongside the Royal Oak pub. To the west is the road bridge to Hayling Island and the stumps of the former railway bridge beyond. Towards Emsworth is the black, cone-capped tower of Langstone Mill, now a private house, which Pevsner aptly describes as 'looking like a lighthouse'. It is in fact a rare example of a Hampshire windmill; Langstone also had a tide mill. Corn was brought to the quay by barge and bread was baked in what is now the pub to be sent to the dockyard at Portsmouth and elsewhere.

The windmill tower at Langstone would almost have certainly fallen down by now if it had not in 1932 been bought by the artist Flora Twort, who is best known for her water-colour paintings of Petersfield Market. Within a few years she had restored the granary and cottage, as well as the tower, converting the latter to a dwelling with the help of the architect Ernst Freud, son of the famous psychoanalyst. During her ownership a stream of creative people stayed at the mill, including Nevile Shute, who wrote his well-known book *Pied Piper* within its walls.

The quay at Langstone is only just above high water and spring tides and strong winds bring risks of flooding. Then the cry that echoes round the cellars of the pub is: 'Get the beer up!' The distinguished writer Victor Pritchett happened to be at the mill in 1937, shortly after its restoration had been completed, when the worst storm in living memory struck the village. He later wrote about it in the *New Statesman*, describing the 'strange white water-light and stillness' that he noticed when everything was battened down that day at Langstone. In the tumult the garden wall of the pub was knocked down and a huge wave 'like a hippopotamus or an enormous gladstone bag' ripped away the verandah of the mill. Most menacing of all, wrote Pritchett, was a wheelbarrow which was being tossed around: 'Down went its bows like a bull's horns, and it charged the house.'

Offshore at the mill lies the wreck of the *Langstone*, a gravel coaster built at Emsworth, which operated from Langstone Quay for many years. The cargo was loaded shovel by shovel from the Winner shingle bank at the eastern approaches to Chichester Harbour, the skipper manoeuvring the craft into a deep pool so that, when the tide ebbed, she would be low enough to make the job of throwing up the gravel as easy as possible.

The Solent Way moves on from Langstone — but do not fail to look back at the scene, one of the prettiest in the harbour. Ahead is **Warblington**, looked over by a prominent octagonal brick-and-stone tower, which stands close to the church of St Thomas à Becket, parts of which are Anglo-Saxon. The churchyard is particularly interesting and

113

Fishing boats at Emsworth.

contains a brick-and-flint gravewatcher's hut in the south-east and
north-west corners. These were used in the early 19th century when,
presumably, bodysnatching was a local concern. There are also many
fine carved tombstones, some of them showing maritime subjects —
such as the burning of HMS *Torbay* in Portsmouth Harbour in 1758,
depicted on a stone to the north of the church tower.

The ruined tower nearby is all that remains of Warblington Castle, a
moated house built around a quadrangle during the early 16th century
by the last of the Plantagenets, Margaret Countess of Salisbury. A
devout Catholic, she avoided conflict with Henry VIII for many years
by living quietly on the Hampshire coast. But at the advanced age of 70
she finally fell foul of the Tudor monarch, who had her executed for
alleged treason, though to the end she denied it.

The path ahead is the last leg of the Solent Way and continues across
Conigar Point, a Public Open Space that takes its name from coney
and is locally called The Bunnies. A mile to the south is the marina at
Northney and the low profile of Hayling Island beyond. Across the
Emsworth Channel to the south-east is Thorney Island, another large

flat island, which until 1870 was separated from the mainland and could only be reached by a wadeway from Emsworth. The waters here are part of the huge expanse of Chichester Harbour with waterways winding to the ancient ports of Bosham and Fishbourne. It is now a major yachting centre and is particularly popular with the owners of large cruisers. At **Emsworth** is a large yacht harbour, much of which makes use of a former timber basin and mill pond.

In the past Emsworth was well known for its oysters and its milling. The town grew up between two enormous mill ponds which were made by damming natural inlets. Water was pounded at high tide and used to power tide mills when the sea fell. Close by the yacht harbour on the east side of the waterfront is the Slipper Mill Pond and the old mill building, now converted into flats. The wheel and the machinery were contained in an extension to the existing structure which ran at right angles above the mill race, and was in use until 1940.

To the west of Slipper Mill is King's Quay, also called Hendy's Quay after Thomas Hendy, who built the mill in the middle of the 18th century. Barges came with corn and left with flour, much of which was sold to the Admiralty at Portsmouth dockyard, which grew enormously in the years leading up to the Napoleonic Wars. The quay, incidently, is on the Hampshire-Sussex border, which here virtually follows the course of the river Ems, which gave Emsworth its name and Slipper Mill the original inlet for constructing the mill pond.

In the last decade of the 19th century Hendy's Quay was used by J.D. Foster, a man whose business interests dominated Emsworth up to the First World War. He was a remarkable entrepreneur who started in business as an oyster merchant in 1875 and later built some of the finest fishing smacks ever to be turned out. The Emsworth foreshore and the waters of the harbour were once riddled with ponds for rearing and storing oysters. The stumps of their wooden structures can still be seen to the west of King's Quay, and there were even rearing ponds built on the tiny Fowey Island a mile offshore — and they are still there.

At one time J.D. Foster had a fleet of 13 smacks from which men dredged for oysters — and scallops — during the winter months. But in 1903 disaster struck: after a banquet at Winchester at which Emsworth oysters were served several guests fell ill with typhus and some of them died, including the Dean of Winchester. The upshot of a scientific enquiry was that the outflow of sewage into Emsworth Harbour had infected the shellfish and no further stocks could be sold. The trade never fully recovered from this setback, even when a new sewage outflow was built.

During his shipbuilding career one of J.D. Foster's quirks was to name the vessels after the initial letters of his name, starting from the end with *Recoil* and ending with *Juno*. No such idiosyncracy formed part of John King's character, a man who gave his name to the shipyard now used by Bowmans Yachts. He came to Emsworth in 1770 and set up a yard which has always been the home of quality and was for many years used by Apps, a famous local shipbuilder. John King's House at No. 19 King Street is well worth seeing. It is a fine black-and-white, weather-boarded house which is said to have been built in a day.

LANGSTONE HARBOUR AND EMSWORTH

The final stretch of the Solent Way runs along the top of a sea-wall which impounds the Seaside Mill Pond on the west side of the harbour. Made in 1760 to serve yet another tide mill, the wall curves round to the shore for 200 yards or more. At the end, and the end of our journey, is the mill building, which is now the home of the Emsworth Slipper Sailing Club. The harbour, with its north wall grafted on to a row of houses from all sorts of periods, is always changing, always full of interest. The tired walker may feel that he has had enough — but for those with the stamina, the intricate waterside of Emsworth, once the haunt of millmen, smacks-men and shipwrights, is as rewarding as any.

And then, at the end of a trail which stretches from Dorset (almost) to Sussex, it is time to rest. And to ask whether there is any stretch of coast with a heritage as varied and as rich as that of Hampshire. Any offers?

INFORMATION

How to get there From Southampton take A35 to Lyndhurst and then A337 through Brockenhurst to Lymington. Continue on A337 to Everton and turn left. Milford on Sea approx. 1½ miles. To Keyhaven turn sharp left on Lymore Lane. Hurst Castle signposted.

Public transport: British Rail stations at New Milton, approximately 4 miles from Milford on Sea and Lymington town. South Wessex Bus Service 123, 124 connects between Bournemouth, New Milton station, Milford on Sea and Lymington. For information telephone Lymington Bus Station, Lymington 72382.

Where to park: Car parks along Milford sea front (parking tickets). Limited free car parking by Sturt Pond bridge. Car parking at Keyhaven (parking tickets). At Lymington by the quay and by the Royal Lymington Yacht Club (also charged).

Where to stay: Wide variety of accommodation in Milford on Sea includes The Red Lion, Bay Trees, Westover Hall, Kingshead Hotel, Rosalyn Hotel, Southdown Hotel and Whitehorse Inn. Needles Guest House, Seaspray Guest House, Compton Guest House. Also caravan and camp sites at Lytton Lawn, Lymore and Seabreeze Caravan Park, Milford on Sea (tents in August only). For an up-to-date accommodation list contact the Tourist Officer, New Forest District Council, Appletree Court, Lyndhurst. Telephone Lyndhurst 042 128 3121 (List, 20p + SAE).

Where to eat: Restaurants and pubs in Milford on Sea village. Beach cafés on sea front. Café at Hurst Castle. Pubs at Keyhaven and Woodside, The Gun and The Chequers Inn. Beaches attractive for picnics, especially by Hurst Castle. Picnic food available from Milford on Sea. Wide range of cafés, pubs and restaurants as well as bakeries in Lymington.

Places to visit: Hurst Castle open all year, but note Keyhaven Ferry Service at present restricted to summer season.
Special visits to Hurst Lighthouse can be arranged with the keeper Mr P. Hobby — Milford on Sea 3970.

Ferry service: Service to Hurst Castle frequent during main season. Also trips from Keyhaven to visit The Needles, and evening outings to Yarmouth. For information telephone Milford on Sea 2500.

Boat launching: Public slipway at Keyhaven. Keyhaven River Warden telephone Milford on Sea 5695.

Swimming: Milford on Sea beach popular in summer for swimming and sunbathing. On Hurst Spit swimming not advised because of dangerous strong local currents. Large open air sea water baths at Lymington near the Royal Lymington Yacht Club.

Cycling route: Use road for Milford on Sea to Keyhaven. Hurst Spit unsuitable and sea walls are public footpath and only wide enough for pedestrians. Ancient Lane from Keyhaven to Lower Pennington possible but beyond is public footpath. Take lane up to the Chequers Inn and turn right on road to Normandy. From Normandy, lanes continue into Lymington.

SOLENT WAY ROUTE: To get to start of Solent Way from Milford on Sea village centre, take Sea Road by Moores Garage, ⅓ mile approximately. Then follow sea front to beginning of Spit by Sturt Pond, ⅓ mile. From here Hurst Castle is about 1½ miles — allow up to 45 minutes (or about one hour from the village centre). In winter or for a short cut cross the footbridge and follow the lane and sea wall direct to Keyhaven. For a visit to the castle plan to spend up to ½ hour. The ferry service runs approximately each half hour. From Keyhaven use the road bridge over the river then continue on shore path. Sea wall now obvious round Oxey Marsh to Eight acre pond (with its sailing club). Beyond this the path follows the sea wall round Normandy Farm to Marina at Waterford. The approximate distance is about five miles so allow up to two hours.

LYMINGTON TO BEAULIEU   9 miles

How to get there: From Southampton take A35 to Lyndhurst and then A337 through Brockenhurst to Lymington. To Bucklers Hard, take A35 to Totton and then A326 to Dibden Purlieu. From here cross Beaulieu Heath and beyond Beaulieu turn left on minor road sign-posted to Bucklers Hard.

Public transport: British Rail station at Lymington town or ferry terminal. South Wessex Bus Services 112 connect Lymington to Hythe via Beaulieu. Summer service 111 between Southampton and Bucklers Hard. For information telephone Lymington 72382.

Where to park: Car parks in Lymington at quay and Royal Lymington Yacht Club (parking tickets). Small free car park pull in by the Burrard Neale Monument. Car parking at Bucklers Hard (charge includes entry to maritime museum).

Where to stay: Variety of small hotels and pubs offering accommodation in Lymington include the Angel Hotel, Anglesea Hotel, Mayflower Hotel, Ramley House Hotel, The Ship Inn, Stanwell House Hotel, Ye Olde English Gentleman, Farino Guest House. Youth Hostel, Norley Wood. The Master Builder's Arms, Bucklers Hard. Montagu Arms, Beaulieu. For up-to-date list of Tourist Board Registered accommodation contact the Tourist Office, New Forest District Council, Appletree Court, Lyndhurst. (20p + SAE). Nearest camp site is Roundhill camp site near Brockenhurst. Forestry Commission site open from mid-April or Easter till end of September.

Where to eat: Wide range of cafés pubs and restaurants in Lymington as well as bakeries and delicatessens serving take-away food. Fish & chip shop and Chinese takeaway. Pub at East End, East End Arms and The Master Builder's Arms at Bucklers Hard has bar food as well as restaurant. Café at Bucklers Hard open during main season. Café in Beaulieu village. Bar meals at Montagu Arms.

Places to visit: Monument at Walhampton open to view at all times. St. Leonards Grange Barn — visible from nearby road at all times. Bucklers Hard maritime museum and village life display open throughout the year (entry charge).

River trips: During main season 'Swiftsure' river bus in operation giving ½ hour tours of the Beaulieu River from Bucklers Hard. For information phone Bucklers Hard 203.

Boat launching: Hard at Lymington Quay. Public slip at Bucklers Hard boat yard. Fee includes car parking.

Cycling route: From Lymington cross old causeway and turn right past ferry terminal (next left for monument). Continue along lane to South Baddesley, and on past Sowley Pond. At junction turn right past Bergerie to St Leonards Farm. Shortly afterwards turn right. Road leads to Bucklers Hard.

SOLENT WAY ROUTE: From Quay Hill take the path through to Mill Lane. Beyond Lymington town railway station continue along Waterloo Road. Cross the river on Bridge Road and then take Undershore Road. Watch out for Solent Way sign up footpath to the monument. From the monument turn right down Monument Lane to footpath across the fields sign posted. After cutting through a small wood, turn left on road by Snooks Farm. Turn right along Bridleway and at junction turn right to rejoin Lymington to South Baddesley Road. From Lymington this is approximatelly 2 miles, say 40 minutes. The Solent Way now continues by road as far as Bucklers Hard. Approximately 4½ miles — allow up to 2 hours. From Bucklers Hard, there is a riverside walk through the woods and fields to Beaulieu village. This sets off from by the landing pier, passes behind the marina and past Keeping Marsh. In Keeping Copse a pleasant path branches to the right following the riverbank. Beyond the former brickworks the route crosses the fields and pastures, entering Beaulieu by the village fire station behind the Montagu Arms Hotel. Riverside Walk, approximately 2½ miles — allow at least 45 minutes.

EXBURY TO CALSHOT

How to get there: From Southampton take A35 to Totton and then A326 to Dibden Purlieu. From here cross Beaulieu Heath to Hill Top and then turn left to Exbury. For Lepe and Calshot continue from Dibden on A326 to Blackfield. Minor roads continue to the coast.

Public transport: Hampshire Bus Service 58 runs from Southampton to Lepe and service 59 runs also from Southampton to Calshot Beach: both in Summer months only.

Where to park: Large car parks for visitors to Exbury Gardens, Lepe Country Park and Calshot Foreshore. Limited area available for parking at Ashlett Creek.

Where to stay: Accommodation for activity holidays and weekends at Calshot Activities Centre (telephone Southampton 592077).

Where to eat: Beach Cafe at Lepe Country Park; teas etc. from Calshot near car park. Cafe also at Exbury Gardens. Waterside pub at Ashlett Creek near Fawley. Large pub at Calshot.

Places to visit: Lepe and Calshot Country Park open all year. Exbury Gardens open April to mid June. Occasional open days Calshot Activities Centre — second hand boat sales etc. Info. telephone Southampton 592077. Also once per year Fawley Power Station open day.

Boat launching: Slipway at Calshot (charged) suitable for dinghies small motor launches and trailor-sailors by arrangement telephone Southampton 592077. Public Hard and quay at Ashlett Creek.

Cycling route: From Beaulieu follow Hythe road up to Hill Top and then road to Exbury, continue on lanes to Lower Exbury and on to Lepe. Continue on road to Stanswood and Ower. Turn right to Calshot or left to Ashlett and Fawley.

COASTAL ROUTE: Coastal path from near Exbury Quay past Inchmery House and Lepe House passable with difficulty. Impassable at high tide. In Lepe Country Park beach closed east of Stansore Point. To continue to Calshot follow lanes inland. Calshot beach open from south of Eaglehurst to beginning of spit. Attractive path by the salt marshes continues to Ashlett Creek.

INFORMATION

BEAULIEU TO HYTHE   6 miles

How to get there: From Southampton take A35 to Totton and then A326 to Dibden Purlieu, from here cross Beaulieu on B3054. For Hythe turn left through Dibden.

Public transport: See ferry below. Hampshire Bus service 112 Lymington to Hythe, Hampshire Bus service 58 or 59 from Southampton.

Where to park: Car parks in Beaulieu village, on Beaulieu Heath and in Hythe.

Where to stay: Hotel — The Montagu Arms, Beaulieu. Dibden Manor Hotel, Dibden. West Cliff Hall Hotel, Hythe.

Where to eat: Bakery/coffee shop, Beaulieu. Restaurant and Cafe, National Motor Museum, Beaulieu. Montagu Arms, Beaulieu. The Travellers Rest south of Hythe. Picnic food available from bakers in Hythe.

Places to visit: National Motor Museum, Palace House and Abbey ruins Beaulieu. Note entrance off Beaulieu-Lyndhurst road 1 mile from village centre. Allow at least half a day for visit. Beaulieu Church — entrance from near riverside.

Ferry Service: Hythe ferry to Southampton — Note, no service on Sundays.

Boat launching: Public Hard at Hythe.

Cycling route: Follow B3054 across heath to Hythe.

SOLENT WAY ROUTE: Solent Way continues from the river to Hill Top (1 mile) and then crosses heath beside road over towards Dibden. From near cattle grid (1½ miles) turn south east following line of pylons along forest edge to roundabout at Hardley, (1½ miles) cross road to Esso depot and then turn north on old tracks and lane. This narrows down to footpath then continues as Hart Hill. Across the level crossing there is a picnic area and shore road brings the walker into the town behind RAF Hythe (2 miles).

SOUTHAMPTON

How to get there: From central Hampshire A33 from Winchester. From west M27 and M271 or A35 from Lyndhurst and south of New Forest. From south east Hampshire M27 and A3024.

Public transport: Good public transport into and out of Southampton by coach, bus and train make the city a good base for walking the Solent Way.

Where to park: Numerous car parks in City Centre as well as metered street parking.

Where to stay: Wide range of accommodation in Southampton. For list contact Information Centre, Above Bar, Southampton. Telephone Southampton 21106.

Where to eat: Wide choice of pubs, cafes and shops selling take-away food.

Places to visit: Maritime Museum, Bugle Street; Tudor House Museum, Bugle

Street; Bargate Museum, Bargate; Southampton Hall of Aviation, Albert Road South.

Ferries and docks cruises: Hythe ferries leave from Town Quay. Note — no service on Sundays. Cruises also around docks and Southampton water as well as to Southsea, Hamble river and Bucklers Hard. For information on arrival of liners contact Southampton Tourist Information Centre, telephone Southampton 20438.

Swimming: Large pool, Central Baths by Western Esplanade.

Tourist Information: Information Centre, Above Bar. Telephone Southampton 21106.

SOLENT WAY ROUTE: The route of the Solent Way is not marked in the City and the suggested tours passing some of the more interesting buildings and museums have been described in chapter. The shortest route to the Itchen bridge is to follow the main road past the Dock gates in Canute Road. Turn left into the Royal Crescent and then right into Albert Road past the new Southampton Maritime Aviation Museum. Steps near this building lead up to the Itchen bridge.

WOOLSTON TO HAMBLE · 6½ miles

How to get there: From Southampton City Centre cross the Itchen Bridge, A3025. To Weston shore, follow Victoria Road, Weston Grove Road and Archery Road. Weston Parade leads out to Netley.

Public transport: Bus services to Woolston Southampton City bus 7 or 9, and to Netley Hampshire Bus 81 or 82. Railway Stations at Woolston and Netley on main Southampton to Portsmouth line.

Where to park: Large car parks at Weston shore. Car parks for visitors to Netley Abbey and Royal Victoria Country Park. Car parks at Hamble and Hamble Common.

Where to stay: Small number of hotels and pubs offering accommodation at Netley. Benfield House Hotel, Victoria Park Hotel, The Prince Consort, La Casa Blanca, Netley. For accommodation list contact TIC, Above Bar, Southampton 20438.

Where to eat: Bakery and take-away restaurants in Victoria Road, Woolston, also in Netley. Park Cafe at Royal Victoria Country Park, pubs in Woolston and Netley. Bakery and pubs in Hamble.

Places to visit: Netley Abbey ruins; Royal Victoria Country Park, Netley.

Boat launching: Public slipways at Weston Point, Weston Shore and Netley. Public Hard outside Royal Victoria Country Park.

Cycling route: Cyclists can cycle from end of Victoria Road, Woolston round to Weston Parade. From here follow road to Royal Victoria Country Park. To Hamble follow road round north of Royal Victoria Country Park.

Swimming: Weston Shore and Royal Victoria Country Park beach are used for swimming at high tide.

SOLENT WAY ROUTE: At the east end of the Itchen bridge take steps down to

INFORMATION

Woolston and continue down Victoria Road to end of road by Sailing Club at Weston Point (1 mile). From here cross recreation ground to rejoin the road at Weston Parade. Walk along seafront and beach past sailing club and Netley Castle Convalescent Home (1½ miles). Turn now across recreation ground and left at road to visit Netley Abbey ruins. If tide is high walk through village to Royal Victoria Country Park entrance (1 mile). In Park follow footpath round the back of the Netley Sailing Club and then road past engineering works. Join beach through wood and continue along beach and waterside, under jetty and then turn left at Hamble Common, (2 miles) where road leads into village. Opposite school turn right down hill to riverside. Ferry 100 yards to south, (1 mile).

HAMBLE TO TITCHFIELD   5 miles

How to get there: From M27 use junction 8, A3024 and B3397 down to Hamble or A27 minor road down to Warsash. Use M27, junction 9 for Titchfield and Hillhead.

Public transport: Bus services from Southampton to Hamble, Hampshire Bus 81, 82 and 85. To Warsash Hampshire Bus 77 and 77A. Bus services to Titchfield Hampshire Bus X16, 77, 77A and 80 from Southampton or Hampshire Bus X16 from Fareham and Portsmouth. Nearest railway station Hound two miles from Hamble.

Where to park: Car parking at Hamble Common, on foreshore in Hamble, at Warsash and at Hillhead. Parking also at Titchfield Abbey and in Titchfield village square.

Where to stay: The Harrier Hamble. Campsite-Riverside Caravan Park, Satchell Lane, Hillhead, Hamble. The Bugle Hotel, Titchfield. Queens Head Hotel, Titchfield. Seven.Sevens, Hillhead. Solent View Private Hotel, Warsash. Bed and Breakfast, Mrs. P. Connolly, 11 Mariners Way, Warsash.

Where to eat: Pubs at Warsash and Hillhead.

Places to visit: Titchfield Haven Nature Reserve — by appointment with the Naturalist Ranger. Booking forms telephone Winchester 64221. Titchfield Abbey ruins.

Ferries and cruises: River Hamble Ferry between Hamble and the riverbank north of Warsash runs every day of the week throughout the year. Summer river trips on the Hamble from Hamble village.

Cycling route: Hamble Ferry carries cycles. From Warsash follow minor roads to Titchfield and then lane down to Hillhead via Meon.

Swimming: Beaches at Hillhead popular for swimming.

Boat launching: Public hard at Warsash.

SOLENT WAY ROUTE: Cross to Warsash on Hamble River ferry. Follow river bank path south past the Rising Sun, path continues on bank and along beach past College of Maritime Studies. Solent Way crosses onto Hook Spit (1 mile) then along beaches to Solent Breezes Caravan Park (2 miles). Beyond this coastal path follows cliff top of Chilling and Brownwich Farms estate. Path drops down to beach at Hillhead (2¼ miles).

HILLHEAD TO GOSPORT   8 miles

How to get there: From Titchfield on A27 follow B3334 to Stubbington and follow signs to Hillhead or Lee-on-Solent. From Fareham and M27 follow B3385 to Lee-on-Solent or A32 Gosport.

Public transport: Bus services to Hillhead and Lee-on-Solent, from Gosport Hampshire Bus 74 and 74A. Bus services to Gosport from Southampton Hampshire Bus X15.

Where to park: Range of car parks near coast from Hillhead to Lee-on-Solent. Car park at eastern end of Browndown and Stokes Bay. Car park for visitors to HMS Alliance Submarine Museum. Free car parks also in centre of Gosport town.

Where to stay: Osborne View Hotel, Hillhead. Seven Sevens Hotel, Hillhead. Belle Vue Hotel, Lee-on-Solent. Ash House Guest House, Lee-on-Solent. Anglesea Hotel, Gosport. Alverbank House Hotel, Stokes Bay, Old Lodge Hotel, Alverstoke. Details of further accommodation including Bed and Breakfast in Gosport from the Tourist Information Centre, Ferry Gardens, Gosport. Telephone Gosport 522944.

Where to eat: Pubs at Hillhead. Pubs, cafes and takeaway restaurants, shops etc. at Lee-on-Solent. Cafe at Submarine Museum. Restaurants, pubs etc. in Gosport.

Places to visit: Alliance Submarine Memorial Museum, Gosport Museum, Fort Brockhurst.

Ferries and Cruises: Frequent foot passenger ferry service from Ferry Gardens to the Hard also Portsmouth Naval Docks, Solent and Spithead cruises from Ferry Gardens, Gosport as well as boat trips to visit Spit Bank Fort.

Boat launching: 3 public slipways at Stokes Bay — public hard at Gosport.

Cycling route: Most of this section is built up with roads following coast closely. Ferries carry cycles.

Tourist Information: Tourist Information Centre, The Ferry Gardens, Gosport. Tel: Gosport 522944.

SOLENT WAY ROUTE: Past the harbour walk along beach or road for first ¾ mile, and then seawalls to Lee-on-Solent (2 miles). Path continues around the beach of Browndown rejoining road at Alverbank. Follow coast round Stokes Bay open space to Fort Gilkicker, (1 mile) then turn inland across golf course to road. Turn right and at car park rejoin sea wall to entrance to HMS Dolphin (1½ miles). Turn left and watch for submarine museum on right. Cross Haslar bridge to enter Gosport town (¾ mile) along shore over new pedestrian bridge.

PORTSMOUTH

How to get there: From M27 follow M275 and then signs to Portsea or Old Portsmouth.

Public transport: Portsmouth Harbour Railway Station services from London, Southampton, Eastleigh etc. Hard Interchange also bus services from Southampton, Hampshire Bus X16, Winchester-Hampshire Bus 69 or 69A to Fareham and X16 to Portsmouth, Eastney-Portsmouth City 15, 17, 18.

INFORMATION

Where to park: Multi-storey car park in Havant Street near the Hard also street parking in Old Portsmouth.

Where to stay: Wide range of accommodation — brochure with full list from Southsea Tourist Information Centre, Castle Buildings, Clarence Parade, Southsea. Telephone Portsmouth 0705 826722.

Places to visit: The Victory, The Royal Naval Museum, Mary Rose and Museum, Domus Dei ruined church ancient monument, Round Tower, Square Tower etc.

Where to eat: Cafe in Royal Naval Museum. Pubs and Cafes along or near the Hard. Pubs in Old Portsmouth and on the Point. Wide choice of pubs and take-away shops in city centre.

Ferries and cruises: Gosport ferry, Portsmouth Harbour cruises and Solent tours from Portsea Pontoon by the Hard.

Boat launching: Public Hard at the Hard Portsea and Old Portsmouth.

Swimming: Popular beaches Clarence Pier to Southsea Castle and all along esplanade to Eastney.

Cycling route: Follow Solent Way route on adjoining roads.

SOLENT WAY ROUTE: From Gosport Ferry landing at the Hard bear right along railway and under bridge into St. Georges Road. Turn right into Gun Wharf Road past entrance to Isle of Wight Car Ferry Terminal. From Gun Wharf Road continue by White Hart Road round the Camber (1 mile). Visit Portsmouth Point along Broad Street, or climb walls and head for Southsea, to south east.

SOUTHSEA AND EASTNEY   4 miles

How to get there: From M27 and M271 follow directions to Southsea or from A27 and Sussex take A2030 down to Fratton and follow signs to Eastney and Southsea.

Public transport: Nearest British Railway Station — Fratton. Portsmouth City Bus services from Portsea and City Centre to Southsea and Eastney.

Where to park: Ample roadside car parking around Southsea Common and along Eastney Esplanade. Car park for visitors to Royal Marines Museum.

Where to stay: List of hotels and other accommodation available from Southsea TIC Tel. 0705 826722.

Where to eat: Beach cafes, pubs, fish and chip shops along esplanades, at Clarence Pier and South Parade Pier.

Places to visit: Southsea Castle, D-Day Museum, Royal Marines Museum, Eastney; Cumberland House Museum.

Cruises etc: Local cruises from Clarence Pier and South Parade Pier.

Swimming: Extensive beaches at Southsea and Eastney.

Cycling route: Local seafront roads.

Tourist Information: Castle buildings, Southsea. Tel: Portsmouth 826722.

SOLENT WAY ROUTE: Promenade from Old Portsmouth continues through or behind funfair and along beaches round Southsea past Castle and D-Day Museum (1½ miles) eventually to Eastney. For Royal Marines Museum join St. Georges road (1½ miles). Entrance to Barracks 500 yards. Otherwise continue on sea front and turn left through to Henderson Road for Pumping Station works, (1 mile).

EASTNEY TO EMSWORTH   11 miles

How to get there: From Southampton take M27 to turn off for A2030 to Southsea and Eastney. For Farlington Marshes watch for entrance on roundabout. For Langstone continue on A27 to junction with B2149 to Hayling. For Emsworth continue on A27.

Public transport: British Rail stations at Portsmouth Airport, Bedhampton, Havant and Emsworth. Bus services from Portsmouth Hard Interchange and City Centre to Eastney, Portsmouth City 16 and 416 and 18 to Farlington Marshes, Portsmouth City 16 and to Emsworth.

Where to park: Parking by Eastney Esplanade, by the Eastney pumping works, by seawall of Langstone Harbour, at Farlington Marshes, at Harts Farm Way, by Langstone Bridge and in South Street Emsworth.

Where to stay: One or two guest houses only at Eastney. For details enquire at TIC, Castle Buildings, Southsea, telephone Portsmouth 826722. Langstone Hotel near A27 roundabout. At Emsworth, Chestnut and Jingles Guest Houses and Hotels: The Crown, Merry Hall and Queens Gate. Also accommodation on Hayling Island. List free from Havant Borough District Council, Civic Offices, Havant.

Where to eat: Pubs by Milton Lock, Langstone and Emsworth. Cafes etc. at Emsworth.

Places to visit: Eastney Pumping Works, Henderson Road, Eastney. Farlington Marshes free access. For information contact Hampshire and Isle of Wight Naturalists Trust tel: Romsey 513786.

Boat launching: Langstone — Hard suitable only at high tide, also public Hard at Emsworth. Public slipway at Broad Marsh.

Ferry: Ferry services from Eastney to Sinah point, Hayling Island — Pedestrians and cycles only.

Cycling route: No attractive cycling route available from Eastney to Emsworth. Follow main roads A2030 and A27, or alternatively cross to Hayling Island and continue north from West Town.

SOLENT WAY ROUTE: From Eastney Esplanade turn left into Henderson Road for Pumping Station. Beyond this cross the small park on the footpath and continue along Ironbridge Lane. Then east down Locksway Road to Milton Lock (1 mile) and Langstone Harbour Shore. Path then continues along harbour shore right up to Eastern Road Bridge by the Tudor Yacht Club (2½ miles).
From roundabout on A27 follow road/track down to Farlington Marshes. Sea wall

path continues right round Nature Reserve (or shortcut available straight ahead) to Eastern corner (2½ miles). Path continues by shore close to A27 passing public slipway before short deviation onto Harts Farm Way, (1¼ miles) and industrial estate. Footpath near mini roundabout returns walkers south west to sea wall round sewage treatment works and eventually to Mill Lane leading through to Langstone Road, (1½ miles). Cross here and follow village street down to Langstone Mill. Follow shore round until path crosses fields to Warblington Cemetery and Church, (¾ mile). Then follow path eastwards to rejoin beach, finally arriving at Emsworth by sea wall round mill-pond, (1½ miles).

FURTHER INFORMATION

Joining The Southwest Peninsula Coast Path: The 17½ miles between Milford on Sea and Sandbanks at the entrance of Poole Harbour, can easily be covered by walkers.

From Milford on Sea follow cliff top walk for approximately two miles but then follow beach to Barton on Sea as golf course is private property.

Continue along beaches beneath cliffs, past Naish Farm Estate to Highcliffe. Continue on to promenade at Mudeford.

From Mudeford Quay ferry services run throughout the year to Christchurch Quay and to Hengistbury head across the mouth of Christchurch harbour.

Paths around Hengistbury Head lead to promenade from Southborne to Pool Head. Ferry service from Sandbanks to South Haven point, Shell Bay, the beginning of the Dorset Coast Path.

Further Walking in Hampshire: The final few miles of Solent Way to Emsworth are shared by the Wayfarers Walk, a seventy mile route across Hampshire which ends at Inkpen Beacon near Newbury. A guide to this walk has been published by Hampshire County Council.

The Test Way also crosses Hampshire from Inkpen Beacon down the Bourne and Test Valleys to Totton on the edge of Southampton, passing through Stockbridge and Romsey. A leaflet guide is available from Hampshire Recreation Department, North Hill Close, Andover Road, Winchester.

Solent Way Holidays: For information on week-long holiday tours of The Solent Way (and other long distance routes) get in touch with Hampshire Recreation Department North Hill Close, Andover Road, Winchester, Hants SO22 6AQ. Telephone Winchester 64221.

Solent Way Video Film: A video film on The Solent Way can be seen at The Royal Victoria Heritage Exhibition at Royal Victoria Country Park, Netley. For information telephone Southampton 455157.

FURTHER READING

Brode, A   *The Southampton Blitz, 1977*

Brown, R   *The Story of Lee-on-Solent, 1982*

Brown, R   *'I remember when it was just fields': The Story of Hayling Island, 1983*

Chitty, J   *The River is Within Us: A Maritime History of Lymington, 1983*

Clark, G   *Britain's Naval Heritage, 1982*

Colebourn, P   *Hampshire's Countryside Heritage: The Coast*

Coles, R   *The Story of Lymington, 1983*

Hockey, Dom F   *Beaulieu: King John's Palace, 1204-1538, 1976*

Holland, A J   *Ships of British Oak: The Rise and Decline of Wooden Shipbuilding in Hampshire, 1971*

Holder, J H   *Explore Hampshire: Its Coast, Countryside and Heritage, 1982*

Joicey, R   *Langstone: A Mill in a Million, 1976*

Jowitt, R L P and D M   *The Solent and Its Surroundings, 1978*

King, E   *Old Times Revisited in the Borough and Parish of Lymington, 2nd ed., 1900, reprinted 1976*

Knowles, B   *Southampton: The English Gateway, 1951*

Light, F W   *A Short History of Warsash, 1939*

Patterson, A Temple *Portsmouth: A History, 1976*

Patterson   *Southampton: A Biography, 1970*

Pevsner, N B L and Lloyd, D   *Buildings of England; Hampshire and the Isle of Wight. 1967*

FURTHER READING

Platt, C — *Medieval Southampton: The Port and Trading Community, A.D. 1000-1600,* 1973

Powell, M — *Spithead: The Navy's Anvil,* 1977

Rance, A B (ed.), — *Seaplanes and Flying Boats of the Solent,* 1981

Rance, A B — *Shipbuilding in Victorian Southampton,* 1981

Rudkin, D J — *The Emsworth Oyster Fleet: Industry and Shipping,* ND

Shurlock, B C — *Portrait of the Solent,* 1983

Titchfield History Society — *Titchfield: A History,* 1982

Titheridge, A — *Hythe Pier and Ferry, A History,* 1981

White, C — *The End of the Sailing Navy,* 1981

White, C — *The Heyday of Steam,* 1982

White, L F W — *The Story of Gosport,* 1964

Widnell, H E R — *The Beaulieu Record,* 1973

INDEX

Baileys Hard	28
Bargate, Southampton	53
Beaulieu	39 43
Beaulieu Heath	43
British Aerospace	64
Brockhampton	112
Browndown	79
Brownwich	73
Buckingham House	94
Bucklers Hard	27
Bursledon	67
Cadland House	33
Calshot Castle spit	33
Canute's Palace	55
Clarence Pier	99
College of Maritime Studies	73
Conigar Point	114
D-Day Museum	100
Domus Dei	96
Eastney Pumping Station	103
Eastney Shore	101
Exbury	31
Farlington Marshes	111
Fawley	36
Fort Cumberland	103
Fort Gilkicker	80
Gods House Hospital	55
Gosport Hard	84
Great Salterns Quay	109
HMS Daedulus	79
HMS Victory	91
Hamble River	67
Hamwih	48
Haslar, Royal Naval Hospital	80
Hayling Island	104
Hill Head	78
Hill Top	43
Hurst Castle	13
Hythe	44
Itchen Bridge	56
Keyhaven Harbour	15
Keyhaven Marshes	16
Langstone	112
Langstone Harbour	108
Lee-on-Solent	78
Lepe Country Park	32
Lower Exbury	32
Lymington	20
Mary Rose	88
Mayflower Monument	49
Mayflower Park	49
Milford on Sea	10

INDEX

National Motor Museum	40
Netley Abbey	60
Netley Castle	60
Old Portsmouth	95
Oxey Marsh	17
Pennington	17
Pylewell Park	25
Royal Marines Museum	101
Royal Naval Museum	90
Royal Navy Submarine Museum	81
Royal Thames Yacht Club	69
Royal Victoria Country Park	61
St Leonards Grange	27
St Michaels Church, Southampton	53
South Baddesley	25
Southampton	46
Southampton Hall of Aviation	56
South Parade Pier	99
Southsea Castle	100
Sowley Pond	25
Stansore Point	32
Stokes Bay	79
Titchfield	75
Titchfield Abbey	75
Titchfield Haven	73
Tudor House Museum	52
Vosper Thorneycroft	59
Warblington	113
Warsash	68
Westgate, Southampton	52
Westfield Common	64
Weston	59
Woolston	58
Wool House Maritime Museum	48

Illustrations

C.C. Bonsey: *102 (upper).*

P.H. Colebourn: *77, 113.*

A.K. Hayward: *12, 15, 24, 37, 41, 44, 47, 79, 80, 81, 84/85, 90, 101, 115.*

J.H. Holder: *Pages 8/9, 11, 16, 19, 21, 28, 29, 33, 36, 46, 57, 59, 61, 65, 68, 94, 97, 102 (lower), 105, 109, 111.*

Imperial War Museum: *72.*

Mitchell Memorial Museum Trust: *56.*

National Motor Museum: *27, 40.*

Portsmouth City Council: *92, 100.*

Southampton City Museums: *49, 50, 52.*

NOTES